The Diaries of
Louis Riel

The Diaries of
Louis Riel

Edited by Thomas Flanagan

Hurtig Publishers
Edmonton

Hurtig Publishers
10560 105 Street
Edmonton, Alberta

ISBN 0-88830-116-2 clothbound
ISBN 0-88830-117-0 paperback

Printed and bound in Canada
by T.H. Best Printing Company Limited

Introduction

Few documents are prized by students of history as much as the diaries of a famous man. They offer glimpses of the diarist when his guard is down, when he communes with himself and forgets his status as a public figure. Such insights give us a living sense of the man's character and personality.

We are fortunate to possess four diaries kept by Canada's most noted opponent of the established order, Louis Riel. Although there are numerous gaps, sometimes comprising several months, the journals contain a reasonably complete record of his thinking during a critical period of time in his own life and in the history of Canada. They begin in June 1884, when Riel was living as an obscure school teacher at a Jesuit mission in Montana, and carry on through the great rebellion of 1885. They also contain entries from a good part of his imprisonment. The record ends about three weeks before his execution at Regina, November 16, 1885.

The existence of these diaries has long been known to scholars, and bits and pieces have occasionally been published or quoted in historical works; but until now nothing like the entire wealth of material was available to the general reader. This volume presents an English translation of all Riel's diaries as a contribution to increasing public knowledge of one of Canada's most remarkable individuals.

One of these diaries was the object of the best known manuscript sale in recent Canadian history. On April 22, 1971, the notebook which Riel kept during the North-West Rebellion was put up for auction. Lost for almost a century, this document had been brought to light in 1970, the centennial year of Manitoba's entry into Confederation, by Eric Wells, prominent citizen of Winnipeg and history enthusiast.

The sale was itself controversial. Mr. Wells did not own the diary; he claimed to be the agent and public representative of the owner, whose name he refused to divulge. Under these circumstances the Provincial Archives of Manitoba declined to purchase the volume, fearing disputed title claims. Mr. Wells then put the diary up for public auction through Bernard Amtmann's firm of Montreal Book Auctions. The actual sale was preceded by a publicity campaign, fed by statements from Mr. Wells and Mr. Amtmann about the value of the diary. Rumours circulated that "wealthy Americans" were prepared to buy this historical treasure. On April 22 two minutes of bidding resulted in a sale for $26,500, high by Canadian standards. The purchasers were a consortium of private individuals whose spokesman was Gene Rhéaume, former member of Parliament for the Northwest Territories and a Metis like Riel. After the auction, Rhéaume acerbically charged that Canada's museums, such as the Public Archives of Canada, were too short-sighted and parsimonious to pay the price needed to keep such manuscripts out of the hands of foreign collectors. He claimed that he and his associates had saved the diary for Canada. The archives replied that they had had a bidder at the auction, that they knew perfectly well what was happening, and that there had never been a real danger that the diary would leave Canada. As I write these words almost five years later, the diary reposes in a bank vault in Edmonton as collateral for the loan used to make the purchase.

While the owners have been looking for an appropriate purchaser, scholars have not had an opportunity to study the original manuscript, and it may be some time before that chance arises. Fortunately the Provincial Archives of Manitoba own a photocopy of the document, made when Mr. Wells brought the notebook there in 1970 to have its authenticity verified. I have used that copy, which is in the public realm, to prepare the translation of the diary presented here. In the case of the other three diaries, there was no difficulty of access to the manuscripts and my translations have been made after study of the original documents.

What of the man who filled these little notebooks with his innermost thoughts? What do we know about him?

Louis Riel was born in the Red River colony, in what is today part of metropolitan Winnipeg. Although he was considered a Métis or half-breed, and always thought of himself as such, his ancestry was seven-eighths white and one-eighth Indian. Riel's family did not lead the roving life of the prairies but was firmly settled in the French part of the colony, where his father farmed, did odd jobs, and dreamed of building a fulling mill. Young Louis, who was intelligent and obedient, soon attracted the notice of the bishop of St. Boniface, Alexandre-Antonin Taché. The lad was given the rudiments of an education in St. Boniface, then sent off at the age of fourteen to study at the College of Montreal. It was assumed that he would return to the North-West as a missionary, the first Métis priest.

But matters did not turn out that way. After several years in the seminary, Louis met a young Montreal girl, fell in love, and decided to marry. He rashly left the college without obtaining his degree, and then his marriage plans collapsed when his fiancée's parents forbade the union. We are not sure why, but it was probably because of his poverty, his mixed blood, or both. Embittered, Riel left Montreal in 1866 — without a wife, without a career, without money. He spent two idle years in the United States and only returned to Red River because the very survival of his family was threatened by the disastrous summer of 1868, when grasshoppers picked the fields clean. As George Stanley, Riel's biographer, has said, he was "almost twenty-four years of age, educated, clever, imbued with a strong sense of pride in himself and in his own people, and unemployed. It was an explosive mixture."

The explosion, which was not long in coming, was touched off by the Hudson's Bay Company's sale of their enormous territories to the new Dominion of Canada. In the negotiations carried out in London, no one thought to consult the inhabitants of the territories. The French Métis, who feared they would come under the thumb of Protestant Ontario, seized the initiative as the impending transfer drew near. They refused to allow representatives of the Canadian government to set foot in Assiniboia until they were consulted about the terms of transfer. Many, though not all, of the English half-breeds and white settlers, who were themselves not overly enthusiastic about union with Canada, sympathized with the Métis.

Louis Riel did not begin this movement, but his political and oratorical gifts quickly moved him to the forefront. He became president of the Provisional Government, which was the only effective authority in Red River over the winter of 1869-70. Sir John A. Macdonald was compelled against his will to negotiate with this upstart youth. Fearing American intervention, the prime minister granted nearly everything demanded by Riel and the Métis: guarantees for the French language and the Catholic religion, an issue of land in recognition of the aboriginal rights of the half-breeds, and the entry of Red River into Confederation, not as a colony, but as a province — the new province of Manitoba. From the Métis point of view, their movement appeared a huge success, and Riel was a hero.

However this general euphoria did not last; one tragic error ensured that Riel's downfall would be as swift as his rise. On March 4, 1870, he had allowed a Métis firing squad to execute Thomas Scott, a prisoner in Upper Fort Garry. Scott, who had participated in two abortive revolts against Riel's regime, was difficult to control in custody, and Riel finally decided to make an example of this obstreperous Orangeman. He apparently felt that an act of capital punishment would accredit his government in the eyes of the world as well as forestall future internal opposition. But the calculation was mistaken. The chief effect of the Scott affair was to cause such hatred of Riel in English Canada that he was never again able to play a full, legitimate role in the politics of the Dominion.

Even as the Canadian government was negotiating with the representatives of the insurgent Métis, a military expedition, under the command of Colonel Garnet Wolseley, was being readied to take possession of Red River. These troops were largely composed of volunteers from Ontario eager to revenge Tom Scott. When they arrived, Riel had to flee for his life. Never again would he be able to feel safe anywhere in Canada.

From 1870 to 1875, Riel led a fugitive existence, sometimes in the United States, sometimes in Canada, but always on the move. The loyal Métis of Red River elected him three times as their representative to Parliament, but he was never allowed to take his seat. Riel waited with mounting impatience for the prime minister to deliver the amnesty which, he believed, had been promised him in the negotiations of 1870. Finally, an amnesty of sorts was proclaimed. Early in 1875, Riel was pardoned for any crimes committed during the Red River uprising, but only on condition of five years' exile from Canada. He who had already wandered five years was sentenced to still another period of the same duration before he could assume his natural position as political leader of the Métis.

Riel could not face life as an obscure exile. He thirsted for greatness, and if he could not have it in politics, he would find it in religion. He began to have visions and revelations, and to see himself as a prophet, a religious founder. He dreamed of establishing a new church, an offshoot of Roman Catholicism, in which the Métis would be the chosen people and he would be "prophet, priest-king, and infallible pontiff." In his vision the Métis were the new Israelites, and he was Louis "David" Riel, their sacred monarch. He proposed to renovate religion by reviving the law of Moses. He wished to return the sabbath from Sunday to Saturday in imitation of the Jews, and to resurrect the Hebrew custom of polygamy.

If Riel had been among the Métis when he elaborated these religious novelties, he might have been successful in founding a new religion; but in fact he was staying with French-Canadian friends in the eastern United States. His friends, stout Catholics all, were appalled at these heresies and concluded that Riel had lost his mind. He was taken against his will to Quebec and secretly committed under a false name to the insane asylum at Longue-Pointe, outside of Montreal. For greater security, he was then transferred to the Beauport asylum near Quebec City. Riel struggled against his captors, but gradually his spirit was broken. Admitting that his cherished ideas were only delusions of an addled brain, he was released early in 1878 and was whisked back to the United States. He had spent almost two years *chez les fous.* Yet the strange and disturbing ideas had not been entirely banished from his mind. Repudiated by his lips, they were still rooted in his heart.

After two years' confinement as a mental patient, Riel tried to establish himself in a quiet, non-political career. He talked of farming in Nebraska; he went to New York to look for work; he travelled to Saint Paul to seek a place in Bishop John Ireland's Catholic Colonization Bureau, helping Catholic immigrants to settle in Minnesota. Because none of his plans led anywhere, Riel grew steadily more desperate. Moreover, he had fallen in love again and pledged himself to marry Evelina Barnabé, the sister of a priest who lived in Keeseville, New York, on the pleasant shores of Lake Champlain. But he could not ask Father Barnabé for Evelina's hand until he could support her in reasonable comfort. And here he was, thirty-five years old, the hero of his people — and a virtual pauper. It was an intolerable situation.

In the summer of 1879, Riel elected for the wilds of Montana, determined to take drastic action. His plan was to unite the Indian tribes of the northern plains for an invasion of the Canadian North-West. His goals were to improve the lot of the Indians, to guarantee the rights of the Métis and to establish himself as a wealthy, or at least a financially independent man. Then he would return east to marry Evelina.

Riel met with Sitting Bull, Crowfoot, and Big Bear. He also intrigued among the Assiniboines, Gros Ventres, and Crows, trying to form a grand confederacy under his own authority. But the Indians were distrustful of this interloper on their prairie, and nothing came of Riel's efforts. For a while, he lapsed into almost total obscurity. He roamed Montana with a band of Métis buffalo hunters, supporting himself as a petty trader. Giving up his dream of returning to wed Evelina, he married Marguerite Monette, a young, illiterate Métisse, and quickly became a father.

By 1882, Riel was beginning to play a role in local politics. He delivered the votes of the Métis to the Republican party and thereby got himself in legal trouble, for neither he nor many of his followers were American citizens. His name began to appear with some frequency in the local newspapers.

In 1883 he renounced his allegiance to Queen Victoria in favour of American citizenship. He also settled down as a school teacher at St. Peter's mission, a Jesuit establishment in central Montana. It appeared that he had finally forgotten about Manitoba and Canada, and would spend the rest of his life in the United States, acting no doubt as the spokesman for the Métis of Montana.

In the meantime, however, events were developing in the Saskatchewan country which would draw Riel back into Canadian politics. Widespread dissatisfaction with certain policies of the federal government led to a unified campaign of protest among all segments of the population — English as well as French, white as well as half-breed. The settlers decided to invite Riel to return to Canada and lead a movement which would defend their rights. A delegation of four men, headed by Gabriel Dumont, was dispatched to St. Peter's mission to proffer the invitation. Riel received the visitors on June 4, 1884. After a day's deliberation, he agreed to come; and he set off across the prairie, transporting his little family and his few possessions in a creaking Red River wagon.

The individual grievances of the settlers were not overwhelming, but taken together they loomed large in the minds of the local inhabitants. They were incensed at the low price of grain following the crash of 1883. They disliked the monopoly of the Canadian Pacific Railway and wanted a rail outlet to Hudson Bay. They wanted the territorial form of government to be replaced by full provincial status. The Métis and half-breeds had numerous complaints about land matters, connected with both the land grant in Manitoba and the absence of such a grant in the North-West. Many of them were also worried about the security of title to their river-front plots of land, which did not fit into the official rectangular survey system. Numerous representations had been made to Ottawa over these and related issues, but without discernible results.

13

Riel pursued a moderate and conciliatory course after his arrival at the village of Batoche around the beginning of July. His policy was to unite all sections of the community behind a petition of grievances to be sent to the minister of the Interior. But Riel also had private, personal objectives which became uppermost in his mind after the petition was completed, signed and dispatched on December 16, 1884. He felt that the Dominion owed him a considerable sum of money for the services and sufferings of his past life. Now he entered into secret and indirect negotiations designed to extract some thousands of dollars from Sir John A. Macdonald. This was, to use an indelicate word, blackmail. Riel offered to leave the country and/or make the Métis do whatever the government wished, in return for a payoff.

Sir John rejected the deal, not so much out of scruples against blackmail, but because he did not think it would work. (He had paid Riel to leave Canada in 1872, but Riel had returned only a few months after accepting the money.) As Riel realized that his scheme would not succeed, he became steadily more radical and started to speak of armed rebellion. A Provisional Government was declared on March 18, 1885, and several hostages were taken with a view to compelling Ottawa to negotiate. By now, almost all the white settlers and English half-breeds had deserted Riel, leaving only his loyal Métis and some Indian allies.

The rebellion was both a political and a religious movement. Riel felt that the time had come to unveil his secret religion to the world. Announcing that he was a prophet, he established the "Catholic, Apostolic, and Living Church of the New World." When the local missionaries refused to accept him as an inspired reformer, he had them put under house arrest. He changed the day of worship from Sunday to Saturday and introduced several other innovations in doctrine and worship. He who had once aspired to be a priest had now gone far beyond that ambition by creating his own church. Although some of the Métis balked at these developments, most seemed pleased to have a church designed especially for them.

As is well-known, the rebellion did not last long. Resistance at Batoche was crushed in four days of fighting, May 9-12. All the Indian bands who had risen more or less independently of the Métis were under control by the end of June. Riel was ineffective as a military leader, chiefly because warfare was not his true objective. He was a prisoner of his past, seeking to force the government to negotiate with him, as he had done in 1869-70. Apparently he did not see that conditions had changed, that the transcontinental railway enabled Ottawa to put a force in the field within weeks. As George Woodcock has pointed out in his recent biography of Gabriel Dumont, Riel brought about his own downfall by declaring a policy of violence and then shrinking from the consequences. He restrained Dumont from the guerrilla warfare which was the Métis' only possibility of military success. Riel preferred to wait at Batoche for the Canadian troops to arrive, even though the Métis and their Indian allies had no real chance of winning a set battle against a modern army. But Riel, of course, hoped this battle would never come; in place of violence, he wanted quasi-diplomatic negotiations with Ottawa. His error was that he pushed the government so far that it could only react with force to reassert the territorial sovereignty of the Canadian state.

After the debacle at Batoche, Riel, hearkening to his inner voice, voluntarily surrendered. He knew he would be tried for treason, but he thought he could turn his trial into a political forum which would embarrass the government and bring about his release. In this expectation, as in so many others that year, he was mistaken. He was convicted of high treason at his trial in Regina and sentenced to hang. His attorneys had entered a plea of not guilty by reason of insanity, and he himself had argued that the rebellion was justified; but neither tactic convinced the jury, which was made up of six Anglo-Saxon Protestants. Appeals went to higher courts, but in vain. Frantic last-minute representations failed to move the federal cabinet to commute Riel's sentence to life imprisonment, even though the jury had recommended clemency. The sentence of execution was carried out on November 16, 1885.

Before he died, Riel re-entered the Roman Catholic church,

abjuring all the heresies he had uttered during the rebellion. Yet he still believed himself a prophet, and he continued to receive visions and revelations. He died believing that he, like Christ, would be resurrected on the third day after his death to save his people.

These brief pages cannot do justice to the puzzling complexities of Riel's character. What was he really? A patriotic hero? A self-seeking villain? A psychotic? A religious visionary? In my own view, the last term comes closest to capturing the essence of the man, but this is not the place to revive controversies about the interpretation of his life. The purpose of this volume is to present Riel's diaries with a minimum of editorial comment, just enough to make otherwise obscure passages intelligible to the modern reader.

What will one learn from these journals, and why are they worth reading? Contrary to the claims that have sometimes been made, these documents, even the highly touted Batoche diary kept during the rebellion, do not contain startling historical revelations. Study of these diaries will not produce a radically new view of the causes, events and aftermath of the North-West Rebellion. In fact, the reader will quickly be struck by how little attention Riel devoted in his diaries to what historians regard as the major issues. Above all, the journals are personal records, and Riel's deepest personal concerns did not always coincide with his public role as politician, statesman and rebel.

The largest single element in these diaries is what I have called "conversations with God," that is, prayers and answering revelations. By this stage of his life, Riel considered himself more a prophet and mystic than a conventional political leader. He was an *exalté*, an enthusiast, an agent of the Holy Spirit. It has sometimes been thought that his religious piety and innovations were merely a sham to gain power over the superstitious Métis; but this is hard to believe after reading these diaries. They show a man utterly convinced of the validity of his personal contact with the Creator.

Some readers will undoubtedly take Riel's prophetic convictions as a sign of mental instability and will interpret his diaries as further proof that Riel was insane and should have been permanently confined in a madhouse. Such a view stems from the metaphysics of the modern age, which terms self-appointed prophets lunatics rather than heretics, and would rather control them by means of the strait jacket than by the stake. But I think that these diaries do not support the hypothesis of mental deterioration. Given Riel's assumption that he was a prophet in direct communication with God, the diaries may be read in a straightforward and lucid way. Their contents are obviously the product of a thoughtful and rational (albeit idiosyncratic) mind. The occasional obscurities arise more from brief entries lacking context than from any intrinsic unintelligibility. As I have tried to show in the editorial comments, many passages which are initially difficult to comprehend can be understood through acquaintance with Riel's love of puns, symbols and allegories. It is not surprising that a man who composed poetry throughout his life would seek to express the secrets of revelation through the manipulation of words.

Beyond the religious dimension, these documents shed light on Riel's baffling personality, which was so full of contradiction and ambivalence. It is virtually impossible to apply any descriptive adjective to him without also simultaneously affirming the opposite. These contradictions are abundantly illustrated in his diaries, where he is by turns exalted and depressed, self-sacrificing and self-seeking, conceited and humble, vengeful and forgiving, courageous and pusillanimous, resolute and hesitant, stoic and hypochondriac. I suppose that all men would reveal themselves as contradictory if we were able to examine their intimate thoughts; but in Riel's case internal ambiguity is so dominant that it characterizes his whole being.

Perhaps a key to these puzzles is found in one observation for which the diaries provide abundant evidence: Riel's life was founded on systematic self-deception. He was, above all, an able and ambitious man who desired glory and recognition. Leadership, whether in church or state, was his lifelong goal. Yet he could not openly admit his consuming ambition, for his theologically well-trained mind knew that pride was the worst of all sins. Hence the need for self-deception; he had to try to appear to himself as a selfless servant of his nation, unconcerned with personal advancement, devoted only to the cause of the Métis. His life became an endless series of dramatic performances with himself as both actor and audience.

One result was a necessary feeling of self-righteousness. Rarely could Riel admit that he had been mistaken in anything of importance. We find one or two genuine admissions of fallibility in these pages, no more. Much more frequent is a kind of pseudo-fallibility, a mock performance of self-accusation in which Riel denounces his sins of gluttony, drunkenness, impurity, luxuriousness and so forth. I call these mock performances because these vices were not really part of his life. He was moderate in his diet, used no tobacco or alcohol, was a chaste and faithful husband, and never came close to living in luxury. His only true fault was his overweening pride — the one defect to which he could not confess without destroying the heroic identity he had laboriously built for himself. His never ending battles with the flesh, his fasting and self-mortification were not real struggles against compelling temptations; they were sham battles against fictitious failings. To use Pascal's famous expression, they were *divertissements,* whose function was to prevent Riel from confronting the stark truth about himself and his ambition.

To say all of this is not to suggest that Riel was a bad man. Far from it. But we cannot pass over his particular kind of self-deception; it is a common trait of charismatic leaders. Their ability to inspire passionate commitment in their followers springs from their total identification of themselves with the common cause. Riel's charisma flowed from the sublimation of his personal ambition into his chosen role of the selfless incarnation of Métis nationalism and the humble instrument of God's will. This was the source of his greatness as well as his ultimate downfall.

History has been fascinated by Riel the leader. Leadership is a mask which conceals, but does not obliterate the human nature of a leader. If we are willing to make the effort, we can remove that mask. That is why I have edited and translated these diaries. They provide an opportunity to become acquainted with Louis Riel, the man behind the hero and the villain of the history books.

Riel's diaries were kept in French except for occasional passages in English or Latin. I have printed the English without change and translated the French and Latin. The translation is, on the whole, more literal than literary. I have tried to give a close English equivalent to the original text and have departed from Riel's wording only where a literal translation would have produced a peculiar effect in English.

The translation may strike the reader as somewhat stilted in certain places, particularly in Riel's lengthy prayers. This is a stylistic feature of the original which I did not feel justified in removing entirely, although I have moderated it a bit. Riel was capable of writing in a lively and direct way, but on religious topics his style tended to become florid and verbose. He was particularly addicted to what rhetoricians call "pleonasm," that is, redundancy. He loved to pile up synonyms, and he rarely used the positive degree of an adjective if he could find a way to employ the comparative or superlative. I confess that I was sorely tempted to cut some of these perorations to make them more palatable to modern taste, but a translation ought to reflect the original, not seek to improve it.

The diaries contain a few poems in French which offer special difficulties of translation. I finally decided to render these into simple English verse. I believe that little literary merit has been lost in the process. Although Riel was a poet of considerable ability, these compositions were obviously written in haste and are not much above the level of doggerel, even in the original.

I have inserted a certain number of editorial notes and comments, which are printed in italics. I have tried to strike a balance between leaving the reader in the dark and supplying so much editorial information that it becomes a nuisance.

A set of biographical notes is also furnished at the back of the volume, containing capsule biographies of all individuals whose names appear in the Riel diaries. If the reader is puzzled about the meaning of an entry which contains a reference to a proper name, he may be assisted by turning to these notes. The information included there is designed to refer particularly to the context in which the name occurs in the text. The biographical notes function as an additional form of editorial comment, relegated to a place where it will be less obtrusive.

Here I would like to acknowledge the help of several institutions and individuals who have assisted in the preparation of this book. The Canada Council and the National Museum of Man have generously given financial support for my research. The Provincial Archives of Manitoba and the Collège de Montréal agreed to allow publication of Riel manuscripts in their possession. Mel Hurtig suggested the project to me. John Bovey gave me invaluable information about the provenance of certain Riel manuscripts. Frank MacKinnon was kind enough to read the introduction and make stylistic suggestions. Glen Campbell helped with difficulties in translation. Several secretaries, but above all Pat Dalgetty, patiently typed and re-typed the drafts of this book.

Finally, I would be remiss if I did not give special mention to two people who have helped me not only with this book but with all my research on Riel: Gilles Martel, of the Université de Sherbrooke, who has generously shared with me the results of his own studies; and my wife, Marianne Flanagan, who has never ceased to encourage my efforts.

The responsibility is mine alone if any errors remain in this book after all the help I have received.

THOMAS FLANAGAN

Calgary, Alberta
March 1976

The Diaries of
Louis Riel

1 Montana
June 1-3, 1884

These few pages are of special interest because they illustrate Riel's state of mind before he was invited back to Canada by the settlers of the Saskatchewan valley. When he made these entries in his diary, Riel was an obscure schoolmaster, teaching Indian children to read and write at St. Peter's mission in Montana. But the very next day, June 4, 1884, when this section of the text breaks off, he was to receive the visit of Gabriel Dumont and three others who had come to summon him to Canada.

In these pages, note how contrary Riel's emotions seem to be. At times he is obviously oppressed by his poverty, his present obscurity, his indifferent health, and his pervasive sense of sinfulness. At other moments he glories in his past accomplishments and in his belief that God has given him a special mission which is not yet played out. The pessimism and the optimism are tied together by Riel's conviction that his current sufferings are only God's means of purifying him for the glory which is to come.

These diary entries suggest most strongly that Riel must have been delighted to be invited back to Canada and must have viewed the invitation as a providential opportunity to regain his vanished greatness.

Sacred Heart of Jesus! I adore You. Sanctify me through and through.

June 1

Archbishop Ignace Bourget is a great saint. He is almost a thousand times holier than Saint Ignatius Loyola. However, he has imitated Saint Peter. After having told me in writing: "God ... has given you a mission which you must accomplish in all respects," he recanted by writing to me several years later that *he had never believed and did not now believe in the mission which I was convinced I had received from heaven.*

But that happened so that his successors and all good Christians would recognize that only the Son of God is truly sinless! Glory then to Jesus Christ alone!

O men, let us beware of ourselves!

O men, fervently pray that everything happens, in spite of our sins, in the way which divine Providence has arranged; and that we do not neglect anything that our conscience bids us do to glorify the Son of God!

June 2

The Spirit of God penetrated my brain as soon as I fell asleep. I woke up saying, "Who has given me this wonderful feeling? Now I am saved."

I nobly defended myself against the man who publicly slandered my character to my face. He wanted to shoot me with his pistol, but he did not dare. I responded to his unfair tirade. I spoke forcefully to him. I felt that he was crushed beneath my strong and subtle arguments. But all that is nothing, if I am not sanctified. I must be holy. Sacred Heart of Jesus, save me. O Sacred Heart of Jesus, grant me the equanimity which is most pleasing to God in the execution of all my responsibilities, even the most difficult.

Sacred Heart of Jesus, if You wish, give me health. Save my soul! Save my body. Let me succeed, conquer and triumph.

Sacred Heart of Jesus! My enemies have trapped me beneath their blows, and I cannot escape. As soon as I regain a little strength, they strike me again. And they relentlessly hold me in the defeat which they have inflicted upon me. Hurry, come to my help. Sacred Heart of Jesus, be my success, my victory and my triumph.

The Spirit of God affects us when He wishes, as He wishes and to the extent which suits Him. He easily exercises his vital influence on us; it is easy for Him to restore our health. Oh, how much good God does for me! He only touches my head and I return to life. Behold, now I am saved.

June 3

The Archbishop of Manitoba [Taché] is still a tainted man [un homme taché]. I see him·in the company of the curé Dugas.

Riel is here indulging in an untranslatable play on words. Bishop Taché he calls un homme taché, *that is, "a tainted man"; and he writes the name of Father Dugas as Du gars, from the word* gars, *meaning "lad" or "stripling." Although the context is not entirely clear, it seems that Riel is recalling the visit he made to Winnipeg in June of 1883. Apparently on that occasion he had a disagreement with Taché about monetary matters, involving "Atkinson" and "McArthur," (see below) who are otherwise unknown. Such a situation is not unlikely; in the course of Louis' long absences from Manitoba, Taché and other priests such as Dugas and Ritchot often acted as his agents in money transfers or petty business dealings. A misunderstanding could easily have arisen out of one of these transactions. For decades after Riel's execution, his family believed that the Archdiocese of St. Boniface owed them a substantial sum of money.*

Upon re-entering Manitoba after a long absence and many sufferings, I said to Father Dugas: "The English are lucky that my health is poor; if it were not for that, I would strike them another blow. I am so weak that the least effort to speak, argue, or persuade leaves me exhausted. I feel a burden weighing upon me. Perhaps my enforced silence will be useful to me some day."

The Archbishop said to me: "When I saw you standing in church, I waited a while before I told you to leave."

I replied, "You really could have said it to me."

We exchanged several unpleasant words. Finally, the Archbishop mentioned the name of an Englishman to me. And he said, "It is he who has your money."

Atkinson, you have my money. I know it from a reliable source.

McArthur, I am confident that you will get my money to me.

Sacred Heart of Jesus! Make Atkinson give me my money, and make McArthur get it to me.

Leader of the Manitobans! Take courage. You see that divine Providence takes good care of you. Because it has told you beforehand what would happen and because it has enlightened you, through its clairvoyant predictions, to help you recover your property.

Leader of the Manitobans! You know that God is with the Métis; be meek and humble of heart. Be grateful to God in complete repentance. Jesus Christ wants to repay you for your labours. That is why He is leading you gradually along His way of the cross. Mortify yourself. Live as a saint, die as one of the elect. Implore the Saviour to spare you at all costs from the pains of the next life. Do not be concerned about your enemies, your false friends who mistreat you. You will see what will happen to them; you will see with your own eyes how some of them will end. Oh, how pitiful it will be! Pray for them. Forgive them.

Take consolation. God wants you to enter immediately the joys of eternal life as soon as you die. Request, seek and find perfect contrition.

Take consolation. God gives you the means to educate your children and to raise them far away from the wicked, in the most pious of sanctuaries, if you wish. There your children will grow up, one day to carry on your interrupted labours, which God will recommence and cause to flourish. Your wife is worthy. She loves you.

Sacred Heart of Jesus! My spiritual director told me at the beginning [of my public career]: "Riel, you will succeed when everyone thinks you are lost." I have believed in his words because of You. I believe that God our Father will fulfill the promise which Your priest made to me. In the name of the Father, in the name of the Son, in the name of the Holy Spirit, I will succeed when everyone thinks I am lost.

Sacred Heart of Jesus! I am lost in an ocean of inextricable complications. For the sake of Saint Joseph and of the Virgin,

Your Blessed Mother, make me succeed. You are the inspiration. Your divine Spirit can easily show me the path I must take to conquer and triumph. Man-God! Bless me according to the intentions of Your Providence, which we love when we do not understand them. Deliver me from the [United] States.

My God! Be my support! My God! Be my support! My God! Be my support!

Sacred Heart of Jesus! In Your mercy and overwhelming love, please bestow upon me the successes, victories and triumphs which are the lot appointed for me by divine prescience, but of which I have made myself unworthy through my sins. O Sacred Heart of Jesus! Sanctify me! Give me the blessings which were destined for me. For the sake of Your name, rehabilitate me! Restore me to the heritage of Your blessings.

Sacred Heart of Jesus! Give me perfect contrition as well as the mortification which You love. Be with me so I can do penance as I ought. Detach me from all things. And please grant me all the precious goods of this life, that I may use them as they should be used, solely in the interest of Your greater glory, for the honour of religion, for the salvation of souls, for the good of society, for my most perfect santification, according to the charity of God's plans!

Oh! Sacred Heart of Jesus, make us really understand that this world is simply the antechamber of eternity. You give us the goods of this life only to put us in the position of more easily being able to win the wealth of eternal life.

June 4

Here the text breaks off.

2 Waiting
Winter 1884-85

After his return to Canada In July 1884, Riel began a period of political agitation to express the grievances of the settlers, French and English, half-breed and white. This activity culminated in the transmission of a petition of rights to Ottawa, dated December 16, 1884. About this time, Riel also contacted Sir John A. Macdonald privately, through intermediaries, to request a cash payment in return for his departure from the country. Thereafter, there was little to do except wait for a reply, both to the public petition and to the private request for money.

Over the winter of 1884-85, Riel did not keep a systematic diary; but he did use his notebook for jotting down various observations and especially for drafting lengthy prayers. These latter are worthy of attention because they illustrate certain persistent aspects of his character. Crowded in among the arid lines of the conventional language of worship, one will find manifestations of Riel's burning ambition to be a saint and a statesman, his oppressive sense of sinfulness, his lust for revenge against his enemies and his firm confidence in providence. Evident in all these themes is Riel's lack of spiritual moderation. His desires are all expressed in absolute terms — perfect sanctity, total victory, complete submission, entire self-abnegation and so on. For better or worse, Riel was not a man to rest content with mediocrity.

In going through these prayers, the reader should also notice a kind of ascending curve of tension and excitement. The earlier prayers, it seems to me, are more formal, conventional, abstract, generalized. The later ones are more concrete and immediate, bearing more closely on Riel's immediate concerns as he began to think of an armed rising. Note the dramatic conclusion to this whole sequence, the sentence from

*the Lord's Prayer, "Thy Kingdom come" — written with a bold hand
in the original manuscript and starkly underlined. This confirms
what we already suspected from other sources, that by the outbreak of
the rebellion, Riel was thinking of himself as the agent of God,
directly empowered to establish His kingdom on earth.*

*Note also that in the course of this sequence of prayers, God begins
to speak back to Riel. Headings like "Avis prophétiques" and
"Prophétie" begin to appear with regularity among the entries.
Whereas prior to this point everything was addressed from Riel to God,
now the Lord commences to answer. This points forward to the diary
Riel kept during the rebellion (chapter IV), which is largely composed
of such prophetic revelations.*

I have seen Bishop Grandin. Several people were with him. He
is coming from St. Albert, he is arriving. He is not far away; it
will not be long until he gets here. He has stopped. His carriage
has stopped with all who accompany him.

*This notation refers to the visit which Bishop Grandin paid to the
Métis in early September 1884. It is the only diary entry stemming
from this time.*

Men can struggle as they will against the will of God and
oppose its fulfillment, but they will never succeed in excluding
it from the guidance of human affairs. God has everything in
His care. Have confidence in Jesus Christ. *It is a providential
event which will save you the same day.*

O my God, remember Your infinite charity towards us. In
Your great love, cast Your eyes on me, my wife, my children, on
all those who are dear to me. Bless us according to the
intentions of Your mercy, which we love even when they are
beyond our measure.

*This last sentence is part of a prayer which Riel composed in June
1884. He was on his way from Montana to the Saskatchewan country,
travelling with his family as well as Gabriel Dumont and the other
Métis who had come to fetch him. When in Fort Benton, he stopped to
receive the blessing of Father Eberschweiler, the Jesuit missionary who
had been his confessor. As the priest gave him his benediction, Riel
said this prayer. The incident had great significance for him, because*

O Lord Jesus, have the charity to grant us, for ever and ever, the remission of all our sins, the remission of all the punishment due to each of our sins. And through Your infinite merits, O You who have received from the eternal Father all power in heaven and on earth, grant us the grace to enter into the joys of Paradise as soon as we have breathed our last.

O Jesus, who died on the cross to redeem us, save us in the greatness of Your charity. Hear us, O good Jesus. My God! If You wish, if You have so decided in Your eternal plans, grant us the grace to live another thirty-seven years, even fifty-one years. Let us detach ourselves perfectly from everything each day while attaching ourselves continually to You. The Missouri River carries a vast quantity of water to the sea: let us offer You a similar quantity of good acts and a similar number of instances of good example to our neighbour.

My God! If You wish, if You have so decided in Your eternal plans, preserve the appearance, the flowering, the strength, the activity and the aura of youth in me for a long time to come. Be kind to Marguerite and me as well as to our children. As they grow up and mature, watch over them for me, we beg You. Grant us, in union with our dear father and mother, brothers and sisters, nephews and nieces, uncles and aunts, cousins and close relatives, our benefactors and friends, the grace to think, pray, understand, comprehend, speak, write, act and serve You in everything, always and everywhere, according to Your Holy Spirit of truth, right, justice, accuracy, true propriety and prompt dispatch, so that we may do much good.

Grant us the grace always to think, pray, understand, comprehend, speak and write in all things according to Your Holy Spirit of precision, conciseness, lucidity, clarity, logic, eloquence, poetry, rich experience and irresistible authority, so that we may work most effectively for Your greater glory, for the honour of religion, for the triumph of truth, for the redemption of the elect and for the improvement of the state of all our enemies.

31

Let me reach my prime at forty and let me retain all the powers of mature manhood until I am sixty. Do not let my hair and beard turn gray and whiten until then.

Please grant us the virtues and the wisdom most suited to our different ages, as well as esteem and respect for everything good in each individual, family, tribe, nation and government.

Please grant us assistance, financial means and the blessings of good fortune for *the Métis, the French-Canadians and the French,* as well as for all children of the Church.

Please grant us for ever and ever Your success, Your victories and triumphs and the glories of a fine and happy old age, so that, after having glorified Your Son and having served You well during a long life, we may have the good fortune to receive here below the most merciful and rewarding application of the merits of Jesus Christ our Lord; and so that, blessed by God and men, we may have the consolation of a peaceful death and the blessing of entering without delay into the delights of eternal life, as soon as we have breathed our last. Amen.

Here is omitted the first draft of a prayer which is largely repeated further on.

My God! If You wish, if You have so decided in Your eternal plans, resurrect Oliver P. Morton as he was and then heal him, so that he may aid us in the United States.

Sacred Heart of Jesus, enlighten us, instruct us, lead us straight to God's salvation, in the affairs of time and eternity.

Sacred Heart of Jesus! Protect us, defend us, sustain us, save us!

Lord Jesus, our loving Saviour! You said to us: "When two of you gather together on earth, whatever they ask, they shall receive from My Father, who is in heaven." Encouraged by Your generous promise, I, Louis David, and Marguerite, whom You have charitably united in the holy sacrament of matrimony and who love You — we are gathered together on earth and we ask Your Father who is in heaven to grant us the grace to seek and to find truth, right, the justice of right reason, the most humble obedience, all virtues and the true Christian spirit of conjugal union for ever and ever. May He have the charity to grant us in addition all earthly blessings such as life, health, liberty, honour, glory, wealth and influence, that we may employ them entirely in Your service.

Please grant us, O Lord Jesus, Your most precious graces. From this day forward, grant us the grace to live in sanctity, to acquire great influence, wealth and a high station in life, so that, while living in comfort, we may never be in the company of wicked men nor under their influence.

Grant us the grace to discover and avoid, now and forever, all the snares and traps which are set for us by the Devil, the world, the flesh and its uncontrolled desires. And let us be protected by Mary; by Saint Joseph, our dear adopted father, the chosen patron of the Métis, the patron of the universal Church; by Saint John the Baptist, the second patron of our nation; by the holy prophets, apostles, evangelists, martyrs and all the saints. Assisted by the merits of Jesus Christ our Lord, we soon may have the good fortune here below to pay all our debts both on earth and in heaven.

Lord our God, You are the father of mercy and of consolation. We are many who hope in You. Do not allow us ever to be cast into confusion. Enlighten us in our doubts, encourage us in our trials. Fortify us in our weakness. Help us in our hour of pressing need. We invoke You; hear us.

We acknowledge Your name; protect us.

Deliver us, because we have placed our confidence in You.

Lord Jesus, You are goodness itself; have pity on the souls in Purgatory. Please come to their relief, please deliver them today, at this very second, in particular the soul of Your servant Marguerite-Marie, if she has need of prayers, and of Your servant Fabien Barnabé.

Lord Jesus, I love You. I love everything associated with You. I even love Your portraits.

Lord, remember me in Your Kingdom.

My faith is strong, but make it even stronger, so that my faith in You may be perfect and that I may receive from You the grace of a peaceful death, if that accords with Your wish.

Lord Jesus, do the same favour for me that You did for the

Good Thief; in Your infinite mercy, let me enter Paradise with You the very day of my death.

Sacred Heart of Jesus, forgive my sins of impurity, forgive all of them, I beseech You, for the love of Yourself. Although these sins are ugly and perverted and most foul, You can forgive me for them completely. Pardon me for all of them in Your admirable power of forgiveness. Pardon all my sins of gluttony. Pardon all my sins of avarice. Charitably pardon all my sins of drunkenness. O Jesus Christ, my most gentle Saviour, pardon my sins of all kinds. And for the sake of the precious blood which You mercifully shed for me, deign to completely remit all the temporal and eternal punishment I have merited through the multitude of my offences. O Jesus, spare me from the pains of Purgatory. With the strongest of all Your keys, close the gates of hell so that its torments do not approach me and so that, saved by the love of Your Sacred Heart and perfectly redeemed and re-created by Your Holy Spirit, I may have the good fortune to be admitted to the enjoyment of eternal life with God as soon as I have breathed my last. O Jesus Christ hear me, I ask You in Your name.

Lord, what should I think of homeopathy?

Homeopathy is a non-scientific system of medical practice which holds that disease may be cured by minute doses of remedies which produce in a healthy person the same symptoms which the patient displays. Riel, who was intermittently troubled with poor health (perhaps ulcers or some other gastric disorder), was obviously casting about for a cure.

At this point a blank page separates the preceding paragraph, written in pencil, from the following texts, written in brown ink.

Lord Jesus, You said to us: "When several are gathered together to pray in My name, I will be with them." Encouraged by Your generous promise, I, Louis "David," and Marguerite, whom You have united in the holy sacrament of marriage and who love You — we unite in Your name to pray that You will be with us. Confident that You are really beside us, we ask God for the grace to maintain a good household, to live a holy life, and to die a most Christian death. I, Louis "David" Riel, ask to find in Marguerite Monette *dite* Bellehumeur a sincere, honest, obedient, faithful, chaste and holy spouse who loves me. She asks to find in me, Louis "David" Riel, a sincere, honest, obedient, faithful, chaste and holy spouse who loves her; so that after having lived a holy life on earth and having raised a holy family (if it pleases You to let us keep the little children which You have chosen to give us), we may have the ultimate happiness of going to heaven to sing God's praises for all eternity.

Obedient Jesus! Grant us the grace to be perfectly obedient.

Jesus, author of life! Sustain us in all the battles of this life and, on our last day, give us life eternal.

Jesus, give me the grace to really know Your beauty! Grant me the grace to really love You.

Jesus, grant me the grace to know how beautiful You are; grant me the grace to cherish You.

Jesus, I beseech You, give me a precise idea, the most complete idea of Your physical beauty.

Give me Your Holy Spirit that I may serve and cherish Him, and that I may cherish Him by making Him be cherished.

Sacred Heart of Jesus, resplendent sun of justice, enlighten us with Your great insight, so that all the steps we take may be good; that all our actions may be well-considered; that our desires, prayers and works may conform in everything to God's pleasure.

Lord Jesus, our beloved Saviour! You said to us: "Anything you ask in My name I will do." Encouraged by Your generous promise, I, Louis "David," and Marguerite, whom You have graciously united in the holy sacrament of matrimony, and who love You — we ask You in Your name to make us a thousand times more obedient, a thousand times more courageous, a thousand times stronger, a thousand times more clear-sighted, a thousand times more capable, a thousand times more adroit, a thousand times more flexible, a thousand times more refined, a thousand times more sincere, a thousand times more honest, a thousand times more temperate in eating and drinking, a thousand times more influential, a thousand times more practical, a thousand times more powerful, a thousand times juster, a thousand times more virtuous, a thousand times more gracious than all our enemies put together, so that we may gain over them Your successes, victories and triumphs, for the rest of our lives. Ever help us, ever guide us Yourself, so that we may prevent the Devil, the world, the flesh and its uncontrolled passions from disrupting the holy Church, our homeland, our nation, our family, ourselves and our little children. Be ever with our benefactors, our neighbours, our friends and our dear relatives; and lead them Yourself in the paths of goodness and truth, through the infinity of Your goodness. O Jesus Christ!

Lord Jesus, our beloved Saviour! You said to us: "Whatever you ask My Father in My name He will give you. Ask and you shall receive, so that your joy may be perfect." Encouraged by Your generous promise, I, Louis "David," and Marguerite, whom You have charitably united in the holy sacrament of matrimony — we ask Your Father in Your name to make our joy perfect by granting us for ever and ever the spirit of intelligence to understand the commandments of God and to do His holy will; the spirit of wisdom to keep us from the world's follies and to act according to right reason in all things; the spirit of strength to conquer all temptations and triumph over them; the spirit of counsel to obey our guardian angel and all those who speak wisely; the spirit of knowledge to know the true will of God as well as the good intentions of those who love us and the malicious plans of those who wish us ill; the spirit of fear to be genuinely afraid of offending God and of improperly provoking other men; the spirit of devotion so that all our prayers and actions may be good.

Lord Jesus! I, Louis "David," and Marguerite, whom You have charitably united in the holy sacrament of matrimony, and who love You — we humbly ask the heavenly Father in Your name to make our joy complete by granting us for ever and ever much faith, much hope, and much charity, as well as deep and thorough contrition for our sins; and by granting us patience, mildness, goodness, forbearance, meekness, modesty, continence, chastity, peace, joy, humility, trust, discretion, gratitude, temperance and prudence in everything — now, throughout our lives, until we have breathed our last.

My God! Your Providence has all things in its keeping. I, Louis "David," and Marguerite, whom You have charitably united in the holy sacrament of matrimony, and who love You — we thank You through Jesus, Mary and Joseph for having taken care to be present until now; and we beg You through Jesus, Mary and Joseph to always take care, if You please, of us both, of our dear little children, of our dear fathers and mothers, brothers and sisters, brothers- and sisters-in-law, nephews and nieces, uncles and aunts, cousins, relatives, generous neighbours and friends; of the vicar of Jesus Christ on earth, of bishops and ordained priests: especially of Archbishop Alexandre-Antonin Taché, of all his archdiocese, of all his clergy, of Father Ritchot, of Father Dugas, of Sister Sainte-Thérèse, and of all the nuns in Manitoba; of Bishop Grandin and all his diocese and of all his clergy, of Father Lestanc, of Father André, and of all the nuns in the North-West.

We thank You for having been with us until now, and we beg You, through Jesus, Mary and Joseph, to always please watch over the soul, the body, the repose and the tomb of our dear Sister Marguerite-Marie, of Your servant Fabien Barnabé, of each of our beloved ancestors, relatives, neighbours, benefactors and friends who are deceased.

Lord our God! Your Providence has all things in its keeping. I, Louis "David," and Marguerite, whom You have charitably united in the holy sacrament of matrimony, and who love You — we thank You for having been with us until now, and we beg You, through Jesus, Mary and Joseph, to always please take care of Your most exemplary and admirable servant Ignace Bourget, of his work, his institutions and of all his clergy; of all the French-Canadian clergy; of Father J.-B. Primeau; of Sister Catherine-Aurélie-du-Précieux-Sang; and of the entire community of Bishop J. B. Brondel, of all his diocese, of his apostolic curacy and of all his clergy: Father Cataldo, Father Palladino, the Jesuit Father Damiani, the Jesuit Father Frederick Eberschweiler who blessed us and our children and

Gabriel Dumont, according to the intentions of Your Providence which we love even when they are beyond our measure; the Jesuit Fathers Prando, Imoda, Giorda, Barcelo, Bandini, and all the Jesuit Fathers; all the Brothers, St. Peter's mission, the patriarch Gabriel Azur and all his family.

We thank You, through Jesus, Mary and Joseph for having watched over the following people until now, and we beg You through Jesus, Mary and Joseph to take care of them always, if You please: my friend William Henry Jackson, whom I have chosen as a special friend, and all his well-meaning followers.

We thank You, through Jesus, Mary and Joseph, for having watched over the following countries until now, and we beg You through Jesus, Mary and Joseph to take care of them always, if You please: all Catholic countries, especially Manitoba, the North-West, Lower Canada, France, Ireland, Italy, Old and New Spain, and all Christian lands, especially Scandinavia and the United States; also the Jewish people, all the Indian tribes that still exist in America, and all the nations of the world; more particularly, the Métis, but *above all*, the French-Canadian Métis.

We thank You, through Jesus, Mary and Joseph for having watched over us until now, and we beg You through Jesus, Mary and Joseph to take care of us always, if You please: that is, to take care of our spiritual and physical health, of the spiritual and physical health of our precious little children, of all our interests and affections, both spiritual and physical, as husband and wife, father and mother, son and daughter, Christians and Catholics.

We thank You, through Jesus, Mary and Joseph, for having watched over all our good efforts until now, and we beg You through Jesus, Mary and Joseph, to always take care of them, if You please: in particular, the task we undertook in '69, and the efforts and labour we are now expending to make the cause of religion succeed in the world; of the effort we have made to stop the ravages of intoxicating beverages among the Métis and Indians of this country; of the attempt we made to denounce the Broadwater Company and Simon Pepin in the courts; of the effort we have made to guarantee the future of the Métis in

Manitoba and in the whole vast expanse of the North-West; and of the political stance which we adopted in Montana in '82.

It was in 1882 in Montana that Riel launched his unsuccessful lawsuit against Simon Pepin and the Broadwater Company for trading liquor among the Indians and Métis. This action brought him into close contact with Alex Botkin, U.S. marshall in Helena, who ran for Congress that year on the Republican ticket. Riel supported Botkin and delivered the Métis vote to the Republicans. This ultimately led to an accusation of vote fraud against him, for the citizenship and voting eligibility of many of the Métis were in doubt.

We thank You through Jesus, Mary and Joseph, for having watched over until now the events great and small which continually occur in the behaviour of individuals, families, tribes, peoples and governments; and for having brought about their logical consequences, consistently and without omission, for Your greater glory, the honour of religion, the welfare of society, the salvation of souls and our own sanctification. We beg You, through Jesus, Mary and Joseph, to always please watch over the events great and small which occur in the behaviour of individuals, families, tribes, peoples and governments; and deign to bring about, consistently and without omission, their logical consequences, for Your greater glory, the honour of religion, the triumph of truth, the redemption of the elect and the improvement of the condition of all our enemies.

Spirit of God our Father, You fill heaven and earth, You are present here and You hear our prayer, You have the charity to keep all things in existence, including ourselves; You dwell in the Pope, bishops and ordained priests in order to *instruct, console, succour, bless, guide and save* the human race, and in the Holy Eucharist to serve as our nourishment and medicine. I, Louis "David," and Marguerite, whom You have charitably united in the holy sacrament of matrimony, and who love You — we beseech You through Jesus, Mary and Joseph, grant us the grace to put to Christian use, for ever and ever, both the good advice and the good admonitions as well as all the good instructions which You have the mercy to give us by means of Your priesthood. Grant us the grace to profit, in a way equally as faithful and Christian, from the necessary nourishment and the potent remedies which You have the charity to give us in the Holy Eucharist. We thank You for giving Yourself to us so often in Holy Communion; for having given Yourself many times directly to our young son Jean; for having given Yourself to our little girl Marie-Angélique, indirectly but effectively, each time that You gave Yourself to her mother who nourished her with her milk.

Let us go to Communion again soon. Come to us, stay with us, abide with us; take complete possession of us in Your infinite mercy.

Speak unceasingly to our conscience to keep us on the right path. Bless us according to the intentions of Your Providence, which we love even when they are beyond our measure.

Lord Jesus! You said to us: "Whatever you ask with faith in prayer, you shall receive." Encouraged by Your generous promise, I, Louis "David," and Marguerite, whom You have charitably united in the holy sacrament of matrimony — together with our innocent children, we beseech You to grant us much faith, hope and charity, as well as perfect contrition; and we ask You, with as much faith, hope, charity and perfect contrition as we can muster in prayer, to send us Your Holy Spirit, who is most just, loving, able and strong; who is most simple, pleasing, engaging, instructive, persuasive, convincing and charming, so that we may work with far-reaching effectiveness for Your greater glory, the honour of religion, our own sanctification and that of our neighbours from one end of the world to another; and so that, with a deep understanding of men and affairs, we may address ourselves to all in a way perfectly calculated to make them work, either unwittingly or willingly, depending on whether they are evil or good, for Your greater glory, the honour of religion, the salvation of souls, the good of society and our own temporal and eternal welfare. Amen.

Sacred Heart of Jesus! I certainly do not deserve Your help, Your support, Your intercession. But because of Your infinite mercy, sustain me, strengthen me, direct me, guide me Yourself in the feelings, affections and actions of the most perfect justice.

Mercifully lead me to the end which You wish to make me attain. O Christ, govern me gently so that I may go to kneel at the foot of Your altar. Rule me so that I may enter the house of Your salvation; make me remain there in piety; be with me that I may follow the light of Christian principles. Enlighten me Yourself so I may stand wholly on the side of the Gospel.

O eternal Christ, make the Holy See be visibly united to Your altar in the New World; let it be, so to speak, the facade, or rather, let it be the greatest, the most elevated and the most certain step leading up to the tabernacle of the living God. O adorable Christ, locate Your Holy See so that it is always among very fervent people; let me keep myself in harmony with Your Holy See, O Christ. O my Lord, let the Holy See and Your altar always support me under all circumstances. May it bless me and save me.

O my God! I beseech You through Jesus, Mary and Joseph, abundantly increase Your life in me. Sustain me, fortify me, heal me. Through Jesus, Mary and Joseph, give me chastity in conformity with Your holiness. Fill me with the purity You love so much.

O Sacred Heart of Jesus Christ, convert us, make us Your purest children. Give me the grace to be truly continent. Sacred Heart of Mary, obtain chastity for us from God. Pray, intercede for us and deign to make us chaste. Make me chaste.

Jesus, Mary and Joseph, implore the divine Spirit of life to forever abound in my heart, brain, stomach, lungs, entrails, in all my limbs and in each of my senses.

O my God! I beseech You through Jesus, Mary and Joseph, in Your infinite power and paternal mercy, please restore me, re-establish my health in soul and body.

Breathe life upon me. Take possession of me. Make my heart young again. Restore my mind. Revive my strength, renew me. Re-make my existence. Flourish within me Yourself; and through the abundance of Your life, so beautiful and lovely, let my soul and body enjoy the most flourishing health, before You and before men. O pure and holy Virgin, bless me, bless my wife and my dear, innocent children.

O my God! I beseech You in the name of Jesus Christ, be in

me like the sap which gives the laurel its glory. Deck me with flowers as You embellish the prairie every spring. Please make me fruitful, even as You now fructify the most fertile and the best cultivated gardens and fields. For the love of Christ, hear me.

Almighty Lord and eternal Father, there is more life in You than there is water in the Pacific Ocean. Have the charity to endow me with just a bit of Your life, and I will be the man with the most life in the world. Send me a single wave of *that water which gushes towards eternal life,* and I will be entirely absorbed in You. Make the flood of Your benediction pass over my head, and I will be forever intoxicated with Your delights and Your life. Jesus! Mary! Joseph! August Trinity! I invoke You. I implore You! Pray for me. Entreat God over and over to descend into me with all the force of His essential love and with all the gentleness of His infinite mercy. O great God! It is easy for You to make me happy, to restore me, to rehabilitate me and to make the sweetness of Your pleasures abound in me more than ever; for I am small. O Father of our Lord Jesus Christ, You are infinitely great; have pity on me for I am infinitely small.

Holy Virgin, Immaculate Mother of the Son of God, ask the Infinite Being to concentrate Himself in my spinal column and to take up residence in the marrow of my backbone, in the marrow of my bones, in my flesh.

O my God, I beseech You in the name of Jesus, in the name of Mary, in the name of Joseph, to reconstitute my soul and body in You; give my entire nervous system more strength and subtlety, more vigour and flexibility than all of humanity possesses.

O my God! If my request is exaggerated and out of place, teach me, let me realize it so I may retract it and address You with wishes in harmony with Your desires. But if my prayer pleases You, deign to heed it and justify it in the eyes of the world. God so good, have pity on us! God so great, take good care of all of us. Heed Your Church, which addresses its prayers to You through me. Hear the voice of the Métis nation which dedicates itself unceasingly to You. Reward the French-

Canadian Métis nation according to its faith in the word of ordained priests and bishops. The Métis have great trust in You, O my God. The confidence of the French-Canadian Métis is unshakeable; it is founded upon Jesus Christ our Lord; Mary the Immaculate Virgin; Joseph their dear adoptive father, the chosen patron of the Métis and the patron of the universal Church; and Saint John the Baptist, the second patron of their nationality.

Lord our God! I, Louis "David," and Marguerite Monette *dite* Bellehumeur, whom You have charitably united in the holy sacrament of matrimony and who love You in union with all the saints of heaven and earth, with the Blessed Marguerite-Marie of Paray-le-Monial and the generous Marguerite-Marie of Ile-à-la-crosse and our dear innocent children — we beseech You through Jesus, Mary, Joseph and Saint John the Baptist to grant us the grace to seek and to find, for ever and ever, throughout the United States, in all parts of their territories, especially in Montana, in the entire Dominion of Canada, in all of New Spain and in all corners of the earth, friends who are very numerous, strong, influential and sincere; friends who, in accord with Your desires, openly and freely take up the defence of the ideas, principles, writings, efforts, words and actions which You inspire in us, so that we may obtain, for ever and ever, Your successes, Your victories and Your triumphs over the multitude of our enemies; and that You may prevent the Devil, the world, the flesh and its unbridled passions from disturbing the holy Church, our countries, our nations, our tribes, our peoples and our governments, our families, ourselves and our children. And please reward us by granting us the favour of being happy in this world and the next.

Lord our God, I, Louis "David" Riel, and Marguerite Monette, whom You have charitably united in the holy sacrament of matrimony, and who love You in union with all the saints of heaven and earth, with the Blessed Marguerite-Marie of Paray-le-Monial and the generous Marguerite-Marie of Ile-à-la-crosse and our dear innocent children — we beseech You through Jesus, Mary, Joseph and Saint John the Baptist to transform our selves, to transform our minds more and more each day; the mind and hearts of our dear relatives, neighbours, benefactors and friends; to mercifully transform John Franklin Forgez, Frederick Sausel, Thomas "de la Dear Born"; to transform the Honourable James W. Taylor, all men of good will, and all those who have some inclination to do good. Deign to grant us all the brightest light of reason and the grace to follow it in everything, always and everywhere!

Deign to bless our marriage more and more each day. Deign to bless ourselves and our dear children. Bless the marriage of our sister Marie-Anne. Deign to bless both her and her husband.

O Lord God, full of charity, we beseech You through Jesus, Mary, Joseph and Saint John the Baptist, mercifully bless Catholic marriage, charitably bless Christian marriage, bless civil marriage and natural marriage as much as You can, so that through the sanctification of conjugal union, Your divine love may give the world generations of men of good will, whose principal ambition will be to work ceaselessly for Your greater glory, the honour of religion, the welfare of society, the salvation of souls and their own temporal and eternal happiness.

Sacred Heart of Jesus! Sacred Heart of Mary! Sacred Heart of Joseph, obtain for us from God, through Your redeeming intercession, the degree of quickness of action which we require in order never to miss any chance of salvation.

Grant us the necessary moderation so that we may never do anything rash. Spirit of God, be my government. Love of Jesus Christ, be my strength and power.

Prophetic Admonitions

You eat a third too much.

Do not be too sure of yourself.

When you eat, do not take any *sweetbreads*. I use this word (sweetbread) to designate everything the Holy Spirit wants to tell you.

Riel is quite possibly punning on the words "les ris," which can

mean "smiles" or "laughs" as well as "sweetbreads." However, I
cannot offer an explanation of what he is suggesting here.

You have medicines with you that you bought without getting proper advice. Do not use them very much. I warn you: if you continue to take them, you will be sick when you get where you are going.

Adopt a regimen. Regulate your way of life.

Eat blood cooked into a good broth. Take it clear. Be careful. Your stomach is weak. Do not eat heavily before you go to bed. Control your appetite when you eat. In the middle of the day, have a good meal of foods suited to your state of health. When you have breakfast, only eat about two-thirds as much as you would like.

Never go out without a hat, whether it's hot or cold.

I think that bean soup is excellent for a person who is run down.

Ripe peas, well-prepared, are good for a weakened constitution.

Corn is a dish that persons whose nervous system has been disturbed should never forget to have on their table.

If you're weak, for whatever reason, procure whatever fruit is in season and nourish yourself with it and you will feel better. Eat currants in currant season, strawberries in strawberry season, raspberries in raspberry season and so forth.

If you can get it, eat sheep's blood for one week, followed for another week by the blood of a cow which has not calfed, then a week of kid's blood, finally a week of poultry blood.

Drink rich milk: sometimes cow's milk, sometimes ewe's milk, sometimes mare's milk, sometimes milk from a she-ass. And if you take care of yourself, you will recover your health, with the help of God.

I commend myself to Jesus, Mary and Joseph, that they may draw down divine influence upon my head. I owe my life to Jesus, Mary and Joseph, for they have preserved me. God Himself affects my brain by exercising His charitable influence upon my brain tissue. He fortifies the marrow of my bones, my backbone. God restores the strength of my heart and the health of my kidneys.

It is God who clears my mind and who restores my body to youthfulness. God makes my blood surge in my veins. Even though I have lived through forty years, it is as if I had never been in poor health. My blood is very warm, I can feel it spread within me. My whole body is warmed as if the sun were burning within me.

O God, Your Power is admirable. You do so much for me, it is as if You were resuscitating me ten years after everyone was ready to bury me.

O Jesus Christ! You have spoken the truth, and You are truth itself. He who expends his strength and his life for You, preserves himself: he happily prolongs his years on earth. And why not? In abiding with God, he abides with life: he lives in spite of death. Saints become sick in order to die ten, fifteen, twenty times. The Spirit of God who accompanies them and who is the spirit of life, unceasingly keeps them alive, to the great disappointment of the wicked.

The wicked live in comfort. It does not take a severe sickness to carry them off. Even their health is a disease, if one keeps in mind their corruption, which is great.

The Lord is in my brain. The Lord is in my heart. The Lord is in my soul. The Lord is in my spirit. The Lord is in all my faculties.

God is in each of my limbs. God is in each of my senses. God perfumes me, He covers my life with balm. God fills my blood with the odour and sweetness of virtue. God remakes all my bones. His powerful hand makes my person grow anew. It heightens my body's physique, by making it more attractive.

He endows me with a constitution so perfect that I have never felt able to move with such harmony and freedom! Oh, how well I feel! I recognize, O my God, that I am Your spouse, the holy Church of the elect. My beauty extends afar like the light which the rising sun casts before itself upon the sea. My glory embraces the world, like the morning star when it gazes upon the equator in the midst of its course.

I am not worthy of Your graces, O my God! But You who

regenerate the one after the other, give me a small part of Your benefits, and I will be healed. My God, You see the bottom of my heart. My thoughts, my wishes and my desires rise towards You like mist from a river. Heed me, for I only yearn for You. I really belong to You. I belong to You a thousand times. O my God, I belong to You a hundred thousand times. O Lord God almighty, I belong to You a thousand million times. I belong to You for all eternity. You have created me for the sake of Your love and Your glory. Save me through Jesus Christ. Save me; Save Your servant Louis "David" Riel. Amen.

Prophetic Admonitions

Do not waste anything.

Riel! Try to provide for your own support. For I do not have the means to see to your livelihood.

Riel! Do not be afraid. Do not compromise the cause of good. And God will lead you as if by the hand.

You will lack nothing; if necessary, angels will come to feed you while you sleep. Pray. Have great confidence in Jesus Christ. And you will never lack anything necessary, until you succeed. And then you will enter into abundance.

Riel! God instructs you about many things. But although you are unusually wise and far-sighted, and even if your intelligence is far above any other, pay attention, be careful. You *must absolutely* pray and go to confession as if you were going to die today. Implore the Virgin Mary to send you the kind of confessor you need; preferably, you should confess to a French-Canadian Métis priest. Because Métis priests are good-hearted, because they are meek and humble before God and man, they are admirably suited to their vocation. All Métis priests are pleasing to God. Pray for them, suffer together with them, but above all follow the guidance of a French-Canadian Métis priest. Métis priests of other origin will not take offence, for they are not envious. It is a command of Providence; they know it, and they are so desirous of seeing the cause of good succeed that in offering you their religious services and in helping you with their money, they themselves will advise you to obtain a French-Canadian Métis priest as spiritual advisor.

This paragraph is not clear. What is a "Métis priest?" A priest who is a Métis, or one who ministers to the Métis? There were in fact no Métis priests in the former sense. All the missionaries in the Saskatchewan country were either French or French-Canadian. So perhaps Riel had the second alternative in mind when he wrote about "Métis priests" or "French-Canadian Métis priests." That would be surprising, however, because on all other occasions when he used the adjectives "Métis" or "Metis-Canadien-Francais" he employed them in the normal way of denoting a person who was a Métis. Perhaps the paragraph refers to the new church which Riel would shortly found, in which ecclesiastical functions would be performed by the Métis themselves.

My God! I beg You please, in the name of Jesus, Mary and Joseph to comfort, heal and long preserve the person who is giving me alms and has asked me to pray for him. Hear me, for Your greater glory, for the honour of religion, for the welfare of society, the salvation of souls, for my own sanctification and for the greatest happiness of my generous friends, in this world and the next.

> O My God, help Thou my fate.
> Rescue me, no longer wait;
> Bestow on me the grace
> Not to frighten men away;
> And teach me how to trace
> The path which is Your holy way.
>
> Support me, so men take
> Me seriously. And see
> That my words in them awake
> Respect for my authority.
>
> Help my friends to heed my warning;
> Let them embrace my plans.
> And make my foes one fine morning
> Scatter in fear before my hands.

Lord Jesus Christ, I beg of You,
Show me Your Sacred Heart, I pray.
Blessed Virgin, Mary so true,
Bid your Son His triumph display.

Oh, let me have such charm
    That in speaking to men,
Both they and their chiefs will open
Their hearts and salute my designs
    Without alarm.

Oh, make me humble toward
All those who would decry me.
And even if they deny me,
Give them a just reward —
    Grovelling, I trust,
    In the dust!

Let me trample the wiles
Of that loathsome band
    Of reptiles.
    Let me tread
    On their head.
And, as I walk the land
    Where evil is rife,
Let me stamp out their life.

Now that Christians are numerous and strong, and now that
the spirit of justice is vigorous in the peoples of the earth, I can
give all kinds of missionaries the following advice: When you
come to a borough or village or locality where Catholics are in
a majority, do not reside with any one person. But assemble the
people for whose sake you are visiting, and ask them if they will
take up a collection to give you your own lodging, together
with your subsistence and other necessities (that is, strict
necessities). If they give you a house which is warm in winter
and sheltered from the summer's rain; if they give you bread,

meat, potatoes and vegetables for your soup; and milk, a good bed, clothes to dress yourself properly, decently, unpretentiously — then stay with them, and Jesus Christ will bless them. But if the people do not give you what you need, pass on. And desolation will not descend upon you, but upon them. God will demand an accounting, above all from the rich but also from the poor, of even the smallest useless or extravagant expenditures. He will tell them: "You have been wasteful. And yet you have nothing to contribute to support the preachers of My word, the Gospel of My Son, and My Commandments! So much for you! Behold the sickness, plague, famine, pestilence, war, frost, hail, drought — the evils which will fall on your flocks, property and families. And if you do not improve, death is not far away: it is approaching, look out, it will soon be on your doorstep. Even today you might see it seated at your threshold. A people which does not take care of its public men, religious or civil, is thrice guilty before God and man."

And you, public men, religious or civil, if you are hard to please, God will punish you terribly. For you commit a sacrilege each time you do not treat a Christian well. Be courageous, all of you, for I have passed through all sorts of trials to save you from evil, or to show you how to escape. All of you, be patient, as I have been, through the grace of Jesus Christ. Or better, be patient as our Saviour was. And it is He who will lead you to eternal life; for He is the only gate, and He alone has the keys.

These reflections may refer to Riel himself. He came penniless to the Saskatchewan country and had to be supported by the Métis. In January of 1885 they actually took up a public collection for him; and it is possible that these words have some connection with that event. If that is correct, then it is interesting to see Riel styling himself a "missionary" rather than a simple political leader.

The voice of my Saviour mysteriously lets me know that I have earned fifteen years of heaven. Oh, if I died, then I would only have to spend fifteen years in Purgatory. Courage, my soul! Almost eight and a half months ago, my God revealed to me that, if I died then, I would owe Him thirty years of Purgatory. In eight and a half months, God has given me the grace to expiate my sins; and His mercy has remitted fifteen years of suffering in the flames of the next life.

Courage! The trials of this world, if they are willingly accepted, are beneficial. Maxime Lépine, who is good and wise and devout, told me an important truth which encourages me: "It is no harder for God to keep alive a weak and suffering person than it is to prolong the days of a strong and healthy man."

Saint Joseph! Our dear adopted father, chosen patron of the Métis! Patron of the universal Church! Pray Jesus and Mary that all the Métis understand me, like me and respect me; that I may make Christian usage of their confidence, and that I give them sound advice about everything! Saint Joseph! Pray Jesus and Mary that all the Métis enter the path of true spiritual and material progress, heart and soul; that they piously receive my good advice, that they ponder it, that they support it by spreading the good ideas with which You have inspired me. Saint John the Baptist, O angelic forerunner of the Son of God! O second but wonderful and glorious patron of the Métis, pray for us.

Saint Joseph! Saint John the Baptist, intercede unceasingly with Jesus and Mary for me and my chief friends, so that, being meek and humble of heart, we may inculcate in our Métis nation all the principles of goodness. Assist us at every moment to win the trust of those who are good, by making them realize their faults, with tact and surprising charity; and by showing them the good side of their character, by strongly encouraging them to walk in the path of salvation.

Prophecy

I am far from Manitoba. All kinds of obstacles oppose my success. But today, February 13, 1885, the Spirit of God speaks to me at daybreak. And transporting me in an instant to St. Vital, He was pleased to let me see and understand what is about to happen. I said to my wife, "Will you be brave?" And without any delay or hesitation she replied, saying, "Yes, I will be calm and reasonable. Go wherever you want." After a little while she said, "Don't be afraid," and a bit later, "And you?" So I must be brave, calm and reasonable like her.

Oh! My God! Grant me the grace to love all my people and all the world. And I beg You, in the name of Jesus, Mary and Joseph, make my love of neighbour truly consist of being meek and humble of heart in all my social relationships. Help me to be very patient with the faults of others; sustain my patience and strengthen it so that I may always be very good toward all my people, toward everyone; so that they may all understand my great desire to help them to correct their faults without rebuking them; rather, that they may be won over by my well-meaning actions; and that my firm resolution to enlighten without coercion be visible to the eyes of the simple as well as of the wise.

Something is wrong. They don't want to embrace you any more.

Lord, what is wrong? And what should I understand by the words, "They don't want to embrace you any more?"

Sacred Heart of Jesus! Obtain for us grace to attract the good men to ourselves. Inspire us so that the religious Irish, the pious Bavarians, the faithful Poles, the wise Italians, the sincere Belgians, the intelligent *Canadiens*, the intrepid and good French and the hardworking and docile Scandinavians be the only ones whose enthusiasm for my plans leads them to leave the United States and come join us in Manitoba and in the enormous expanse of the North-West.

O God, because of this immigration, we beg You in the name of Jesus, Mary, Joseph and Saint John the Baptist to mercifully keep wolves, bears, bison and other wild animals away from us. Grant us for ever and ever the most respectable and holy settlers — *Thy Kingdom come.*

3 Insurgency
March 1885

Around March 1, 1885, Riel began to speak publicly about taking up arms; and on March 19 the Provisional Government was declared. In the interval, Riel was apparently too busy to keep a systematic diary — understandable, perhaps, but a great pity from the standpoint of the modern historian who would like to know more about what went on at this time. For there is a great deal about the outbreak of the North-West Rebellion which is still not entirely clear, particularly the extent to which Riel either led or was led by events. The fragmentary material Riel did insert in his diary at this time contributes nothing to resolving that question, although it does illustrate the inextricable involvement of the political and religious themes with which Riel confronted the Métis. From the beginning the rebellion was as much a religious as a political movement.

If they do not want to (here the Spirit sighed), make the freighters leave.

O my God, if You wish, if You have so decided in Your eternal plans, I beseech You, through Jesus, Mary, Joseph and Saint John the Baptist, make them wish [to leave].

Alas! . . *(page torn)*.

The French-Canadians of the United States do not have the relative number of public jobs which they deserve, considering the proportional influence which they exercise at election time.

Father Fourmond reads me a paper, and he begins by saying, "Listen, Monsieur Riel."

O my Métis people! You complain that your lands have been stolen. Why, how can it be that you have not yet recovered them? You hold all the cards, you are strong enough.

All you have to do is take your lands. The foreigner cannot resist you. Pray God to grant you His Spirit; and the moral force of His wisdom, together with the divine courage of the Sacred Heart of Jesus, will make you surmount all difficulties.

O Sacred Heart of Jesus, help the Métis people to take up arms; help them to use them well, and to gain Your successes, victories and triumphs. O Holy Virgin! O our Lady of Lourdes, Mother ... *(text breaks off)*.

On March 5, there was a secret meeting between Riel and a group of ten militant Métis, half of whom were allied to Gabriel Dumont by ties of blood or marriage. Riel drew up the following revolutionary oath, to which all the men affixed their signatures.

We, the undersigned, pledge ourselves deliberately and voluntarily to do everything we can to
1. save our souls by trying day and night to live a holy life everywhere and in all respects.
2. save our country from a wicked government by taking up arms if necessary.

May God the almighty Father help us. Jesus, Mary, Joseph, Saint John the Baptist, intercede for us! Pray for us unceasingly, so that we may gain your successes, your victories, your triumphs, for ever and ever; for these are the successes, victories, and triumphs of God Himself.

We particularly pledge ourselves to raise our families in a holy way and to ceaselessly practice the greatest trust in God, in Jesus, Mary, Joseph and Saint John the Baptist and in all our patron saints. For our banner we take the commandments of God and the Church and the inspiring cross of Jesus Christ our Lord.

Joseph Ouellette	his mark	X
Gabriel Dumont	his mark	X
Pierre Gariépy	his mark	X
Isidore Dumont	his mark	X
John Ross	his mark	X
Philippe Gariépy	his mark	X
Auguste Laframboise	his mark	X
Moïse Ouellette	his mark	X

| Calixte Lafontaine | his mark | X |
| Napoléon Nault | his mark | X |

After several blank pages comes this prayer, which is not part of the preceding oath:

Lord our God, through Jesus, Mary, Joseph and Saint John the Baptist, allow us, in this month of March in the year eighteen eighty-five, to take the same position as we did in '69; and to maintain it most gloriously for Your sovereign domain, most honourably for religion, most favourably for the salvation of souls, advantageously for society, and most suitably to procure in this world and the next the greatest sum of happiness for all those who will help us directly and even indirectly. Change our clergy, as well as Charles Nolin and William Boyer. Transform all of us together.

4 Rebellion
March~May 1885

During the rebellion, Riel kept a very regular diary. He seems to have begun shortly before the engagement at Duck Lake (March 26) and to have continued through the battle of Batoche (May 9-12). The document is of extraordinary importance for understanding Riel's frame of mind during these historic events. It touches on themes too varied to be gathered together in these brief introductory remarks, so I will insert explanatory remarks as needed throughout the chapter. Here I will simply point out that the diary largely consists of revelations and communications from God, together with prayers and reflections. It has occasionally been suggested that Riel's religious fervour was a cynical piece of play-acting designed to hoodwink the superstitious Métis; but such an opinion is hardly tenable in the face of this evidence. If Riel had been merely playing a part, he would scarcely have bothered to record his pseudo-revelations in his diary. The fact that he did record them shows that he felt them to be genuine and of deep significance.

The Spirit of God informed me that a battle had taken place about two miles this side of *Duck Lake*. This was not told to me in words, but was communicated to my spirit in a more tangible way than is usually the case with a simple thought. I am convinced that an event of this kind has occurred, for it was revealed to me that the *Crees* had rendered us a great service there. The divine communication ended more precisely, saying, "You will give Tchekikam whatever he asks of you."

This entry would not seem to refer to the well-known battle of Duck Lake, which took place on March 26, for Riel was present at that engagement. However, the day before there was also an altercation near Duck Lake between a small party of police and a group of Métis under Gabriel Dumont. Blows were exchanged and shots were fired, but there were no casualties on either side. Riel's "revelation" probably refers to this event, at which he was not present.

The Spirit of God spoke to me about the police. My God deigned to tell me: "If you miss them by that road," (The Holy One pointed to the road which runs in front of St. Anthony's Church and then rises), "you will still have time to catch them. You will just have to take them on the hill." (The Spirit of God showed me the hill above Batoche.)

The Spirit of God made me hear the voice of Michel Dumas saying to Riel, "Your ideas are right."

The Spirit of God made me see that I could get to the battlefield ahead of time by myself. I was off to one side. I had some equipment brought to the field under cover. The Spirit of God warned me that the enemy planned to make an effort to take me prisoner.

O my God! Help me, guide me so that I do not do anything rash. Do not let me confide in anyone unless it is reasonable and proper. Assist me, direct me, so that I do not jeopardize the cause. Support me, that I may remain free, that I may come and go as necessary, that I may succeed, that I may conquer, that I may triumph in the name of the Father and of the Son and of the Holy Spirit.

The Spirit of God made me see a crate full of merchandise. On the bottom were written the words, "The heart of the North." O my God! For the love of Jesus, Mary, Joseph and Saint John the Baptist, grant me the grace to conquer the North and to master all within it: give me the heart of the North.

The Spirit of God made me hear the voice of the recruits, who were telling me, "Shoot first; we have never yet fired on the enemy."

The Spirit of God told me in English what spirit should preside over the movement: *generous, unanimous.*

The Spirit of God told me an important question for me to ask the fighting men: They haven't seen any Indians, I suppose?

I saw a flight of dark geese. They seemed to soar; but in reality they were motionless in the sky. I saw them divided, as if in two groups. The leading goose who, with the others, was heading west, suddenly turned left and went east. The geese were in the sunshine, but they did not reflect the light. They were covered with darkness. You warriors who fight for the sake of evil principles, you are like the black geese. God will halt you in mid-flight. And in spite of everything, you will lose your way. Hear, pay attention, obey: and you will escape from the setbacks, the defeats and the shame that weigh you down.

The Spirit of God made me see Father André. He was very small. He turned his back on me. He wanted to get away from me, but he could not. He was very narrow-minded.

The Spirit of God said to me, "The enemy has arrived in Prince Albert."

I prayed, saying, "Please let me know who this enemy is." The answer came, "Charlie Larance."

The Spirit of God showed me the place where I would be wounded: the first joint of the ring finger. While pointing out the joint with His own finger, the Spirit told me, "I think that you will be wounded."

I saw a sheet of paper written in French which began with these words, "Don't you know someone by the name of Charlie Larance?"

He wants to drink five gallons in the name of the movement.

He is offering to raise the Indians by using liquor.

The Spirit of God made me understand that we should tie up the prisoners.

I really think that Edouard Dumont's trip to Fort Lacorne is going to do some good, and that he is going to intercept the fugitives from Prince Albert who want to escape by steamboat.

The younger Dumont did succeed in returning from this trip with a handful of Métis volunteers to help defend Batoche.

I saw Gabriel Dumont. He was troubled and ashamed. He wasn't looking at me. He was looking at his table which was completely bare.

But Gabriel Dumont is blessed. His faith will not waver. He

is steadfast through the grace of God. His hope and confidence in God will be justified. He will emerge from the struggle loaded with booty from his enemies. Jesus Christ and the Virgin Mary will make him happy again.

My ideas are right; they are well-balanced. They are level and clear; there is no mourning in my thoughts. My ideas are like the sights on my rifle. My rifle is upright. It is the invisible presence of God which holds my rifle straight and ready.

I went to a meeting with Maxime Lépine and another man. I saw myself in the mirror of justice. Good sense shone in me; it shone, it sparkled in my face. Lépine did not seem to be paying attention. He kept away from me. He did not leave me, but he was not listening carefully. Maxime! Maxime! It is human respect, it is self-love which is killing you by destroying your good intentions.

The Spirit of God made me see seven or eight young Métis who came running towards me. They wore no coats. Their shirts were of clean, blue and white striped cotton. The one in front ran at full speed. They are earning their salvation, they are concerned with their salvation. You might think they were playing tag, but they are not playing: they are saving themselves, gaining paradise. They are winning the land that others want to take from them.

Through the mouth of one of my French-Canadian Métis brothers, the Spirit of God spoke the following Cree word to me: *Ayoco.*[1]

I saw a large number of our people lying in ambush. J.-B. Boucher was with us. We were waiting for the enemy. All at once two large wagons arrived. I shouted to our volunteers who were on the other side of the river. I thought they were being taken by surprise. But that wasn't the case, for someone said, "It's Larocque."

The Spirit of God told me, "Our people are not numerous. They must be carefully placed and supervised."

---

1. The exact significance of *ayoco* is uncertain. Professor Stan Cuthand of the Department of Native Studies, University of Manitoba, suggests that it may mean "that one" or "that's it."

The following entries concern Riel's efforts to establish a new religion for the Métis. Under his urging, the Provisional Government or Exovedate (from the Latin words ex, *"from," and* ovile, *"flock") passed several resolutions which meant a break with the Roman Church. Specifically, Riel was officially declared a prophet, Bishop Ignace Bourget was named pope of the New World, and the Sabbath was transferred from Sunday to Saturday in imitation of the Hebrews, the first chosen people. Not all the Métis welcomed these innovations, as is shown by Riel's references to the opposition of Maxime Lépine and Moïse Ouellette.*

O my God, I beg You, in the name of Jesus, Mary and Joseph, please sustain me within myself, please sustain me in the Exovedate, please sustain me in the army. As You are my sustenance, sustain me. You alone can do it. O please turn the entire army and Exovedate against Maxime Lépine. Grant me the grace to treat him kindly and with humility, but sincerely and frankly, that he may change his conduct and overcome his campaign of opposition. Because of the charity he has shown towards me, give him a chance to return gracefully to all the ideas which You inspire in me.

O my God! Grant me the grace to re-establish Your day of rest, so that men will again honour the Sabbath day, as determined by Your Holy Spirit in the person of Moses Your servant.

O Jesus, Mary, Saint Joseph, Saint John the Baptist! Pray for us, pray for me before the Almighty that the Métis people and I may do the will of God our Father, that I may accomplish my mission in all respects.

Show them, O my God, that I do not act alone. O Jesus! Act for the glory of our heavenly Father, while I proclaim His word aloud.

O Mary! I do not deserve that God should guide and help me. But for the love of Jesus Christ, beseech Him to continue His perfect guidance and His victorious and triumphant assistance.

O Jesus, Mary, Joseph and Saint John the Baptist, change the obstinate mind of Moïse Ouellette. In Your mercy, make

61

him freely and gracefully acknowledge that it is *permissible* to leave the Roman Church. Beg God graciously to touch his heart so that he will devote himself entirely to the divine reform of the liturgy and to overcoming all the deficiencies in the religion which Rome has inculcated in the peoples of the earth.

O please hear my prayers, O my God, for the sake of Jesus Christ our Lord, through the protection of Mary, through the patronage of Saint Joseph and Saint John the Baptist.

Father J.-B. Primeau told me, "God will grant you everything you ask Him." I ask You to fulfill his promise, for the sake of Jesus Christ. Make all the members of the French-Canadian Métis Exovedate support my mission completely. Without exception, let all the members be nobly, piously and religiously in favour of the complete accomplishment of my mission.

O give all of us the foresight, the prudence, the courage, the strength and the plans we need to finish what we have begun and to do Your holy will in all respects.

O my God! I beg You, through Jesus, Mary, Joseph and Your servant Saint John the Baptist, give me, give to all the French-Canadian Métis Exovedes and to all those who have volunteered for Your cause, the grace to act for ever and ever deftly, expeditiously, immediately, quickly and harmoniously for Your greater glory, for the honour of religion, for the salvation of souls, for the good of society and for our greater happiness in this world and the next.

While I was praying, the Spirit of God showed me a small boat on the south branch of the Saskatchewan. There were two or three men in it. One of them wore a red tuque. They were going down the river, keeping near the left bank.

At the same time, or a little later, the cable of the ferry looked to me as if it were broken in two. It seemed also that the police were coming from Troy.

Be careful at the crossing: set up a close watch, both day and night.

The Spirit of God conversed with me about the events of the battle. The volunteers were all courageous; everything went well.

Bravery means being ready to do God's bidding in all things, always and everywhere.

On April 6, during the night the Spirit of God [appeared to me]. In eight days Taillefer, the noble captain of the Eternal City, will present arms at Sainte-Thérèse. And twenty-four hours later, he will be at Montreal, at nine o'clock in the morning. The Spirit of God let me know by means of His Angel that the appearance of Captain Taillefer was an act of Providence to celebrate the installation of Ignace *Pierre* Bourget as bishop of universal jurisdiction.

April 5, 1885, was Easter Sunday. Riel is interpreting the Easter celebrations in Quebec, in which the Papal Zouaves, commanded by Captain Taillefer, played a ceremonial part, as the inauguration of his own new religion. In Riel's thinking, Bishop Ignace Bourget of Montreal was to be the new pope, a fact which he emphasizes by attributing to him the name of the first pope, Peter.

The bullet grazed me — O my God! Ward off the wound which I am in danger of receiving. Please inflict it on one of my enemies who arrogantly carries a cane or wears a gold ring on his finger. Let the bullet graze him but spare his life.

Spirit of God our Father, O You whose power and charity are infinite, You whose presence fills heaven and earth, who are here now, who hear my prayer, whose goodness keeps all things in existence, including ourselves: I beg You in the name of Jesus Christ, mercifully bless this bread and drink. Into the former, infuse the abundance of the essence of bread, which is in You; in the latter, concentrate the copious essence of milk, in which You are rich. Change this terrestrial bread and drink into a heavenly bread and drink, so that in eating this bread I may eat the best substance to be found on earth; and in drinking this cup, I may drink the milk of divinity; and by rejoicing at this banquet, I may also rejoice at the banquet of eternal life. Through Jesus Christ our Lord.

I see a troop of forty or fifty men camped on a hill; they are keeping watch. They are the pickets of the enemy army. They are not far away. They are northeast of here. They are pickets who are looking for bread. They are made of dead and dry wood.

Riel, the irrepressible punster, is playing on the word piquet, *which, like the English "picket," means either a military sentry or a wooden stake. That the enemy soldiers are only "dead and dry wood" shows that their cause is lost.*

I see people, horses and wagons who are leaving the Saskatchewan country; they are heading east.

I see people, oxen and wagons making for Fort Lacorne. They are Indians who are leaving us.

I see a large herd of domestic animals. They are all red and piebald and light in colour. They are being hastily driven towards Prince Albert.

Spirit of God our Father, whose power and charity are infinite, whose presence fills heaven and earth, who are here now, who hear my prayer, whose goodness keeps all things in existence, including ourselves: mercifully bless this bread. Make it abound in the essence of bread which is in You, so that by infusing Yourself into this earthly bread, O my God, You will make it into a heavenly bread; and so that in eating it, I may eat spiritual and divine food which has the power to create in us good and pure flesh, like the very flesh of the body of Jesus Christ; and so that in receiving it properly, I may receive the bread of regeneration, the most potent universal remedy, the essential nourishment, the sustenance necessary to the health of my soul and body.

O my God! I firmly believe that through Your power, for the sake of Jesus Christ, You have blessed and consecrated the visible nature of this bread and that You have bountifully added to it Your corresponding divine nature, so that by eating it I absorb the *spiritual flesh* similar to the substance which You used to create the body of Jesus Christ. And I am assured by faith that in eating this consecrated bread, I nourish myself with an excellent substance which is no different from the substance of the body of Jesus Christ. Thus in going to communion I receive flesh similar to the flesh of your Son! Thanks be to You, my Saviour!

Spirit of God our Father, whose love for us is infinite, who can do whatever You wish, whose presence fills heaven and earth, who is here now, who lends an ear to prayers which are sincerely addressed to You, and who has promised to hear my pleas: I give You thanks in union with Jesus Christ my Lord for the countless benefits which You unceasingly confer upon us.

It is You who preserves the existence of all the living beings that You have created, who change inanimate things or leave them as they are, as it pleases You. You are the fundamental substance of this drink. Bless it, in Your mercy. Deign to fill it with the essence of milk which is in You. Change this earthly milk into heavenly milk, so that in drinking it I may find a drink thousands of times richer than all the beverages of earth; and so that in slaking my thirst with it, I may absorb the spiritual and divine liquor which has the power to create in me good and pure blood, like the blood which fills the heart and veins of Jesus Christ, who has risen from the dead and ascended into heaven.

O my God, I firmly believe that through Your power, for the sake of Jesus Christ, Your beloved Son, the consecration of this milk has made it delectable, so that in drinking it I drink the milk of Your divinity and in slaking my thirst with it, I quench myself at the fountain of eternal life.

The communion of the New Testament is a communion of gentleness and strength. It is full of life.

O Blessed Virgin Mary, you are the queen of the Eucharist.

O Saint Joseph! You are the great protector of all those who desire to nourish themselves with the body of Jesus Christ and who are changed by drinking His sweet and precious blood.

O Saint John the Baptist! Glorious patron of the French-Canadians and the Métis! Praise be to you for having suffered death and having generously sacrificed yourself in the cause of purity. O great precursor of the living Son of God, you soar amidst the elect on the wings of prayer and penitence. Intercede for us, so that the Lamb of God will take away our sins and anoint us with the balm and perfume of purity, through the communion of His living and life-giving body.

There is some uncertainty as to the precise meaning of these several entries which seem to refer to a Holy Communion of bread and milk rather than of the traditional bread and wine. During the rebellion

Riel established his own religious ceremonies, although we do not know whether a Eucharistic service was included among them. If it was, the substitution of milk for wine would have been a natural step for Riel, who, in addition to being a lifelong teetotaler, was troubled with a digestive ailment which led him to drink a great deal of milk.

O my God! I beg You in the name of Jesus, Mary, Joseph and Saint John the Baptist, forgive the mistakes which I made among the Crees, Sioux, Blackfoot, Bloods, Saulteaux, Sarcees, Assiniboines, Gros Ventres, Piegans, Nez Percés, Pend d'Oreilles and Flatheads. Deign to send them all to help me. May Your mercy bring them from the rising sun! May Your charity lead them swiftly on the wings of the wind which comes from the setting sun. May Your power send them quickly to us from the north! May Your Providence dispatch them to us from the south! O my God! Through Jesus, Mary, Joseph and Saint John the Baptist, let them arrive very soon, provided with good weapons and a large supply of ammunition.

The Indian tribes mentioned are those whom Riel attempted to unite in Montana in the winter of 1879-80 for an invasion of western Canada. Obviously he hoped that his earlier efforts might now bring results.

O my God! I beg You, in the name of Jesus, Mary, Joseph and Saint John the Baptist, please remember Aldéric Ouimet and all the French-Canadians with Middleton. Oh, incline their hearts and souls in my favour, in favour of Your work. And in the midst of battle, have the limitless charity to save them and to save us, by inspiring them with the magnanimity to throw down their arms or make peace with us.

April 19

I hear the voice of the Indian. He comes to join me, he is coming from the north. He is in the mood for war.

I see five horsemen coming down the hill. They are riding at an angle to the river. They are on the south branch on the east side. There are two in front, then comes one by himself; his horse is spotted, light-coloured, almost piebald. The last two are side by side. I think they are hiding. These riders are Métis, judging by their horses.

I see a large number of Indians, they are on the other side of the river. They are single file, they are following our path, most of them are in a hurry. Every day new Indians come to increase their number, they have the same purpose as we do. Courage, my people, courage.

If Joseph Delorme had been out scouting, it seems to me that he would have been caught or surprised. God wants you to keep order here. Do not go scouting too often, not whenever you feel like it, but only when you are told to go and when you have learned not to ask for the job.

O my God! You have taken me under Your special and paternal protection because I begged You to, for the love of Jesus, Mary and Joseph.

I was not able and I am still not able to succeed against our enemies without Your divine assistance.

I am hampered by my own faults, by the faults of our friends and of the whole nation. But we are all Yours; we offer You our lives. For the sake of Jesus Christ, pardon all our faults, all our sins.

Open to us Yourself the path to success, the road to victory, the broad highways of the most complete and brilliant triumph. We beg You in the name of Jesus Christ, the Blessed Virgin, Saint Joseph and Saint John the Baptist.

Make up for the faults of my guards by mercifully notifying me through Jesus of things which happen which they neglect to inform me of, even though they should.

Charitably give me the information and the advice that my friends cannot give.

Open to me Yourself the route I need to send our messengers to the United States. It is already late. We no longer have the human means we once had. O my God, let us know the route our messengers should take. And if there are none open, clear one Yourself in Your goodness. And deign to guide them there by the hand.

April 20

O my God! I beg You, for the love of Jesus Christ, protect us from any kind of betrayal, from death, from wounds, from even the slightest injuries.

Please take care of Your servant Michel Dumas, that he may receive no wound or injury. Do not let death come near him! And because You are all-powerful and merciful, please make the evils with which he is threatened descend upon his armed enemies. O my God, I am saying the same prayer for all the Métis volunteers, who are dedicated to defending truth, justice and right and who have consented to take up arms for the love of the Good Lord and of His loving Son. Forgive their reluctance, take good care of all of us, as You are great and good.

O my God! Take good care of Norbert Turcotte. Prolong his life, please; station him in battle so that he is out of danger. Shield him with Your protection, inspire me to do Your will. O Jesus, Mary, Joseph and Saint John the Baptist, pray God to help me in the fullness of His gifts.

O my God! I beg You, in the name of Jesus, Mary, Joseph and Saint John the Baptist, please use our ferry cable to overturn the steamboat so we may gain possession of all the provisions and useful things in the boat, like weapons and ammunition.

General Middleton had equipped the steamer Northcote *to be a supply ship and gunboat. The Métis plan was to stop the boat by raising the ferry cable at Batoche's Crossing. The scheme was actually tried; but as the hawser was lifted too high the only result was that the vessel's smokestack was torn off.*

April 21

I have seen the giant; he is coming, he is hideous. It is Goliath. He will not get to the place that he intends to occupy.

I see him: he is losing his body, he is losing all his men. Nothing but his head remains. Because he will not humble himself, his head is cut off.

Not surprisingly Riel, who had adopted the name "David," saw the enemy as "Goliath."

The Spirit of God spoke to me of La Belle Prairie and the people who ought to stay there.

"La Belle Prairie" was the local Métis name for an area slightly east of Batoche. Actually, Riel wrote "la jolie Prairie," but I am assuming he meant the former name.

O my God! I beg You, for the love of Jesus Christ, in consideration of Your Immaculate Virgin, in honour of Your special friend Saint Joseph, and in exaltation of the angelic John the Baptist, break the communications of our enemies. Do not let them understand one another or agree with each other; let them move in confusion! O my God! Grant us the favour of meeting them in such a way that we can defeat them one after the other. In Your mercy, let our battles come at times far enough apart so that we will be well-prepared and in a strong position. Let us open fire at the time and place which the charity of Your Holy Spirit has determined in our best interest. If You wish, if You have so decided in Your eternal plans, send us Irvine twenty-four hours before Middleton, and Middleton twenty-four hours after Irvine. Send us the steamboat when we can deal with her at our leisure.

O my God! Hasten, be quick, have the goodness to make the Crees arrive right away to help us win, to help us triumph.

I beseech You, in the name of Jesus Christ, the Blessed Virgin, Saint Joseph and Saint John the Baptist, hear me! Send us the forces we need immediately; send us the Crows and the Blackfoot and all the Indians we need to accomplish in all respects the work we have been given to do.

O my God! I beg You in the name of Jesus, Mary, Joseph and Saint John the Baptist, withdraw Yourself from the children of evil, that they may abandon themselves to the false and malevolent advice of the fools who flatter them. Make the anxiety and the terrible fear of death grow in them after taking

69

away their life's last resort. Weigh upon them. Upset them internally. Strike them with stupefaction so they arrive at the moment of battle not like soldiers but like men condemned to death, like criminals convicted of their enormous guilt, who come to be executed by letting themselves be guided by the deceptions of praise and human approval; like guilty men, like robbers and murderers whom the hand of God encompasses, whom His justice frightens, whom the weight of His wrath crushes, and who start to reel as soon as the fight begins; so that as soon as they hear the thunder rumble they will know that the Almighty is getting ready to inflict the punishment and pain of retribution upon them.

April 22

Hear the words and the lamentations of one who wanted to fight against us: "Furtively I came with an army to hurl myself upon the people of the Saskatchewan country. I found myself trapped in loneliness, outside the settlements, among people whom I pretended to help but who did not want me.

"Suddenly I heard the sound of the Indian braves, formed into one army. They were many, they were united. I heard them singing with great strength and harmony. My army was frightened. They could only think of running away, of finding safety in flight. But neither they nor I could save ourselves. Alas! Alas! War is great and solemn for those who wage it for the love of truth, justice and righteousness. Alas! Alas! War is horrible for those who are not just. Woe! Thrice woe to soldiers who fight on the side of evil; they are soon vanquished."

The Spirit of God told me: "You are right. Protect your families, protect them in the things of this world and of the hereafter." And I repeat over and over, protect your families in the name of God. Guard them from armed danger as well as from the perils of scandal. Guard them from the scandal of corruption, protect them from the horrors of mortal sin.

April 23

I awoke with a start.

April 24

The Spirit of God showed me the upper road. It is open, it is clear, it is wide. I do not see any sign favourable to the enemy. The upper road is a fine road. It is the road of the Métis who are marching toward victories here below. It is also the heavenly route which leads the souls of those whom the Lord has chosen on the battlefield to Paradise.

April 25

On April 24, an inconclusive engagement was fought at Fish Creek. Gabriel Dumont and his men surprised General Middleton's column and inflicted heavy casualties before withdrawing. This battle furnished the major subject of Riel's diary entries for the next several days. On the one hand, he was obviously pleased that the Métis had acquitted themselves so well and that Middleton's cannons and Gatling gun had been ineffective. On the other hand, Riel knew that the Métis, while gaining time, had not yet won a victory. He declared four days of fasting and penance to ask for God's help in the coming struggle.

The Spirit of God showed me Middleton's cannon; it is overturned. It is evil because it directs its fire against the throne of God. The carriage is separated from the barrel. The barrel itself is broken in two. Middleton's gun is broken into three pieces. However, the three pieces are still holding together. But it does not take much to split them completely apart, the first from the second and the second from the third. It does not take much effort to remove the carriage from Middleton's cannon for good and to break the barrel of Middleton's fine gun into two separate pieces, completely apart from one another.

O my God! I beg You, for the love of Jesus Christ, in the name of Your Immaculate Virgin, in the name of Your Saint Joseph and of Your Angel, Saint John the Baptist, guide events so that Middleton's army remains checked and does not recover from the setback it met yesterday on its road of pride. Because Middleton's gun aims its fire against Your Majesty's throne, have the charity, O my God, to keep it broken in three as it is now, to conclude the battle that Jesus Christ waged against it yesterday. You are infinitely good, O my God! Please separate the carriage and the barrel of Middleton's cannon as completely as possible. Separate them forever, O my God! You Yourself have broken the barrel of that big gun into two pieces. Finish that break. Let it be irrevocable and irreparable. Let the break in the barrel be a mortal blow.

"O my Métis Nation! For a long time you have offended Me with your horse races, by gambling on these detestable races, by your obstinacy, by your odious wrangling about your wicked horse races. That is why," says the Eternal Christ, "I killed your horses yesterday while sparing you."

The Eternal One remembers the sinful attachment you have to your horses; that is why He greatly diminished their number yesterday. "The next time I ask you to let Me use the horses I have lent you, you will not refuse. O my Métis people! I am only punishing you lightly. All I ask from you is obedience."

Although the Métis lost only five men at Fish Creek, fifty-five of their horses were killed by enemy fire.

April 26

Middleton's army fired at me awkwardly with their cannon. It did not do me any harm. Thank You, O my God, for having protected me so well. Middleton's troops have given me a cannon, they have put it at my disposition. O my God! Grant me the grace to take it and make use of it. Oh, through Jesus Christ my Redeemer, through the Blessed Virgin Mary, Saint Joseph and Saint John the Baptist, be with me so I do not miss this chance to have a good cannon, one or two, two or three cannons in my possession, with all the ammunition we need.

I saw the Touronds above me. Several of them were wounded. I said to them: "You too? Take courage! You are playing an important role. God will make use of you and your children."

O my God! Protect the Touronds! Save the life of all of them, please. May Jesus Christ please keep them safe. May Mary please sustain them. May Saint Joseph please intercede for them with God! May Saint John the Baptist serve them as an intercessor before the throne of the Lord.

The Spirit of God showed me the enemy tents. I saw no one around. Middleton's tents were beginning to appear on the hilltops. Where are those who have set them up? Are they sleeping? Are they hiding? Have they run away? O my God! Grant me the grace to find them. Oh, would they sneak into the woods to try to infiltrate among us during the night, or unexpectedly during the day? Preserve us from that misfortune, O my God! But if that is their plan, grant us, for the love of Jesus Christ, the Blessed Virgin and Saint Joseph, the good luck to discover them in time to defeat them and triumph over their evil plans.

O my God! I beg You, for the love of Jesus Christ, in the name of Mary, in the name of Saint Joseph and Saint John the Baptist, take away from our enemies that guile, that finesse, that animal cunning which only aims at evil, which has nothing good in it. O my God! Hear me! Take away from all our enemies their skill, their deceit and their means of concealing their movements from us. Assist us to discover them. Help us surprise them even while they are trying to surprise us. Oh, make them bring about their own downfall. Lead them astray, scatter them, do not let them regroup their forces. Let them stay lost in the woods like rabbits and hares. O my God, mock those who mock You.

Speaking of the Métis nation, the Spirit of God told me: "I am going to get angry with them, for they are too negligent. They are not vigilant and obedient enough."

O my God! Do not punish the Métis Nation. For the sake of Jesus, Mary and Joseph, have mercy on them. See how charitable they are, how meek and easy to lead. O my God, take into account the great tasks which the Métis Nation is performing for Your greater glory, for the honour of religion, for the salvation of souls, for the welfare of society.

O my God! I beg You, for the love of Jesus, Mary, Joseph and Saint John the Baptist, do not get angry with the French-Canadian Métis Nation.

Instead, turn Your wrath against Your enemies, O my God. Inflict an extraordinary and terrible punishment upon them, in Your infinite mercy for Your children.

O my God! In Your charity You said to me, "I am going to get angry with them." Please get angry with the Mounted Police; oh, get angry with them! I accuse them before You, in the name of Christ whom they blaspheme, in the name of the Virgin whom they insult, in the name of the Holy Spirit whom they offend by blaspheming the holy sacrament of Baptism. Punish the Mounted Police dreadfully. You are going to get angry with them because they are entirely opposed to Your Holy Spirit of justice, to Your Holy Spirit of right, to Your Holy Spirit of truth. For the love of Jesus Christ, for the love of Mary, for the love of Saint Joseph, save us marvelously.

April 27

The Spirit of God spoke to me in His mercy; He condescended to inform me that "they said 'yes' too quickly."

O my God! I beg You, for the love of Jesus, Mary and Joseph, please make up for the fact that the Métis Nation said yes too quickly. Have the charity to make me know what I have to do to prevent Your wrath from descending upon them.

O my God, look with favour upon the way Your people are fasting and praying to gain Your favour. Oh, help them bitterly regret the error they made in saying yes too quickly. Oh, bless the fast of Your children! Inspire the prayer of Your people. Accept the desire they have to please You. Oh, pardon their sin. Today, at this moment, lead into Paradise those whom You have chosen in battle and whose spirit You have called to Yourself.

Please comfort and heal those among us who have been wounded in battle. Unite their sufferings to those which Jesus Christ endured for all of us.

April 28

The Spirit of God who is infinitely good and to whom I continually give thanks told me something consoling. I cannot remember the exact words He used, but I can announce the good news for Him; for *help is coming to us.* The Spirit of the Good Lord even condescended to let me know that *He was rushing this help to us.*

On May 1, Joseph Jobin arrived with a message of support from Poundmaker's Crees. In the margin next to the above prophecy, Riel had him enter the following note to attest that the prediction had come true:

May 1, 1885 — Fulfilled to the letter. I am the messenger bringing word of this assistance and I can say that God has helped me and is helping me to make this assistance come quickly. Jos. Jobin.

The Spirit of God told me, "When the Crees arrive, be sure to stay away from their women." At the same time I was thinking of Michel Dumas.

The Spirit of God showed me that I had a wooden log beneath my feet. I gave it several blows with an axe. After about four blows, it seemed to me that I was no more tired than if I had only taken two swings. I hardly noticed them. And yet I had made terrific cuts in that log, in that big aspen I had beneath my feet. I will keep it under my right foot while I remain with my axe in my hand.

The Spirit of God made me see that the Métis wanted to go home chiefly because of their wives. And this pure and grand Spirit of love inspired me to speak to them man to man: "Your wives are no dearer to you than mine is to me."

The Spirit of God made me see a passing shadow that disappeared before my eyes. I hardly had time to see it.

When I close my eyes, I see a light brighter than the light of the sun.

April 29

The Spirit of God made me see the Métis Nation in the likeness of Jeneviève Arcand. She was not quite as tall as Jeneviève. Her face was anything but attractive. One could read there the unmistakable signs of sensual over-indulgence. She loved the pleasures of the flesh; the thoughts, the desires, the considerations of the flesh were what occupied her most. But she was travelling in the path of justice. She did not want to stray from it. She purposely went to great lengths to convince me of her love of justice. And when she was able to show me her great attachment to the truth, she was satisfied. She was genuinely proud of showing me how much she cared about right reason. But she was still horribly disfigured by her liking for carnal pleasures.

Suddenly I saw her transformed. She had kept herself much too far away from me for a long time. Oh, how glad I was to see her come back to me! She faced me squarely. She grew; in a moment she acquired the most remarkable strength and stature. At the same time her face was re-shaped. Although it could not yet be called pretty, it was much better.

Oh, who can tell what changes fasting and prayer can produce in a people of good will! Properly performed, four days of fasting is enough to turn a nation of dwarves into a nation of giants.

O my Métis Nation! Take courage! Your four days of fasting, prayer and mortification have produced wonderful effects of transformation among you. I see your change; it is great.

Religion lifts you up. The more you lend your support to truth and religion, the more truth and religion will make you great, strong and powerful.

The Spirit of God made me see that I was with my wife in the house of our French-Canadian race; I had a place in the dwelling of my Father. But that place did not make me feel entirely at home. I only saw my wife from time to time. Nevertheless we were happy, because our morals were chaste and continent. Nothing came to disturb our nuptial bed. My wife lived in grace, and my life was fulfilled in loving her. And if it is true that my family's only coat of arms was a single rosary, at least I had the consolation of finding it to be one of the great attractions of the fatherland. Men did not often seek out my table. In compensation, those whom I invited to it were good men. My clothes were of linen. Yet I passed my days in a kind of rapture; the delights of my life meant more to me than material treasures. And when my wife came and went, I did not worry about her. I had nobody to fear.

Oh, what a blessing it is to be among an honest people! Oh, how happy you are when you have confidence in those with whom you live.

The Spirit of God made me see that I was going to the battlefield. I saw that some of my men were late; they were lagging behind. I let myself be held up. I was concerned about my wife. Without my advice, she had gone to stay in the house which was furthest removed from the fighting. I suspected that she might encounter bad company there. Oh, how hard it is to wage war! O my God! Guide me, help me in war, that I may have the good fortune to conclude a peace in accord with Your intentions, an honourable peace before God and men.

The Spirit of God placed me in a cart with Michel Dumas. He was leaving for the United States. I drove him some way while we talked about the United States. I do not remember the words I said nor the ideas I expressed. But I ended by saying to Michel Dumas, "Think of me as an example for yourself."

Riel actually wrote this last sentence as "regardez-moi comme un exemple Tibi." Instead of completing the sentence in French, Riel wrote and underlined the Latin word Tibi, which, as the dative case of the second person singular pronoun, means the same thing. Why would he suddenly shift to Latin? At a guess, he may have been punning on the English phrase "to be." He did something similar at his trial, when he played on the similarity of "t'aider" and "today." But this is admittedly conjectural.

Incidentally, this passage makes it appear that Michel Dumas left to fetch help from the United States; but we know from other sources that Dumas was at the battle of Batoche and only afterwards left Canada. Perhaps he started to go to the United States at this time, but for some reason turned back.

I left him, I returned, and he went on. As I watched him go along the trail, I noticed a large flowered snake following him. This snake was alone and had no others with it, but it was large. I did not think much of it. I turned around to go back to where I came from. An area around me was clear and open; all the rest of the ground swarmed with snakes. There were more snakes than I could count. Oh, it is a dangerous step to ask the Americans for help. Beware of adventurers from the United States. For I assure you they are to be feared. They have neither morals, nor faith, nor heart. They are dirty dogs, foul jackals, ravishing wolves, raging tigers.

O my God! Save me from the misfortune of getting involved with the United States. Let the United States protect us indirectly, spontaneously through an act of Your Holy Providence, but not through any commitment or agreement on our part.

I used to live wretchedly in the United States among serpents, amid poisonous vipers. I was so surrounded that wherever I wished to set foot I saw them teeming. The ground was crawling with them. The United States are hell for an honest man. A respectable family is in disrepute there. It is ridiculed, scoffed at. Oh, what a great misfortune it is to be obliged to go seek refuge in the United States.

O my God, for the love of Jesus, Mary, Joseph and Saint John the Baptist, grant me the favour of speedily reaching a good arrangement, a good agreement with the Dominion of Canada. Oh, mercifully arrange everything that this may be. Guide me, help me to secure for the Métis and Indians all the advantages which can now be obtained through negotiations.

Grant us the grace to make as good a treaty as Your charitable and divine protection and favourable circumstances will permit. Make Canada consent to pay me the indemnity which is my due, not a small indemnity but an indemnity which will be just and equitable before You and men!

Bless me in my choice. My God! Guide events Yourself.

These last paragraphs are most revealing. They show that Riel, although he had declared a Provisional Government of sorts, did not really intend to overthrow or break away from the Canadian state. Rather, he hoped to force the prime minister, as in 1870, to negotiate the grievances of the Métis as well as his own personal claims.

April 30

The Spirit of God told me to *foresee a mutiny.*

The Spirit of God made me know that a delegation was arriving. It was composed of three men in whom I did not have confidence. Tom Mackay was part of it. The members of the delegation displeased me. I did not like the three men of which it was composed.

O my God! Through Your Providence, You take care of everything; take good care of us. Guide us, help us to make the best of this delegation if You see fit to permit it to be sent to us. Oh, for the love of Jesus Christ, of the Blessed Virgin and of Saint Joseph our great patron, and for the love of Your angelic John the Baptist, give us the grace to turn against the government at Ottawa all the traps and snares it intended to set for us by sending us such a delegation, composed of Tom Mackay plus insignificant persons.

I saw men dressed in dark blue cloth. They did not seem to be armed. They were coming down from the height of their finesse [*meaning obscure*]. The first one came down alone, then they came two by two. Are they soldiers? No, they are students.

I see the masts and rigging of a boat which is going down the river; it is going fairly quickly.

May 2

I see a good number of Métis sitting peacefully on the grass. They are together, they are next to one another, they are sitting in line. Nothing can disturb them.

The Spirit of God has made me sense that my righteous actions were mixed with certain feelings, certain views which tarnished the whiteness and innocence of my soul.

The Spirit of God has given me His holy approval and has praised me for having clarified religion by declaring that it means:

1. to have great confidence in God and in Jesus, Mary, Joseph, Saint John the Baptist, etc.

2. to observe the commandments faithfully.

3. to pray unceasingly and to have devotion.

Priests have been ordained to support the spirit of religion. They have authority only in as much as they are faithful to their mission. As soon as they stray from that, they have lost their position and their usefulness. Priests are not religion.

The Spirit of God told me that that was true, is true, and always will be true.

Riel's new religion naturally meant an open break with the Catholic missionaries. To prevent them from undermining his leadership, Riel collected all the priests, brothers and nuns and put them under a form of house arrest. At the very time when he made these rather anticlerical comments in his diary, he was engaged in vehement efforts to persuade the missionaries to abandon Roman Catholicism and come over to the "Catholic, Apostolic and Living Church of the New World." These efforts were unsuccessful; and so for the brief life span of the new church, priestly functions devolved upon the laity.

May 3

Oh my God! Send the torrential flood of Your loving and merciful blessing upon me, upon my wife and children, upon the Exovedate, upon my whole nation. Do it, I implore You, for the love of Jesus, Mary, Joseph and Saint John the Baptist.

O my God! I humbly ask You in the name of Jesus Christ, in the name of Mary Immaculate whom we particularly honour during this beautiful month,[2] and in the name of Saint Joseph: fill our French-Canadian Métis hearts with the most perfect faith and the greatest confidence in Your Holy, Catholic, Apostolic and Living Church of the New World. On each member of the French-Canadian Métis Exovedate, send down all the charitable gifts of the priesthood, all the evangelical graces of the ministry, all the wonderful fruits of Your Holy Spirit, that each Exovede may be pleasing to You, that each may celebrate the solemn and consoling services of the true religion, edifying Your people in grace! Come to all of them, abide with each of them, live in the very centre of their souls, take total possession of their being so they may receive from You the power to forgive the sins of those who confess to them and to take away the weight of sin from whoever does penance to their satisfaction and implores Jesus Christ for the spirit of repentance.

2. May is the month of Mary in the Catholic liturgy.

As Middleton's troops drew nearer, and a last battle became inevitable, the Métis, still Catholics at heart, naturally wished to confess their sins before risking their lives. To satisfy this need without recourse to the missionaries, Riel instituted a form of lay confession in which the Métis confessed to one another and particularly to members of the Exovedate, as suggested by this paragraph.

May 4

The Spirit of God made me see two fighting men; they were walking down from Prince Albert. There was something big in front of them. I don't know what it is. But I can tell you that it's nothing good. The two men are not together. One is coming behind the other. They are not going very fast. The purpose of their mission is evil. They are trying to cause a great deal of trouble and confusion. But they are not achieving the goal they have in mind.

Evening of May 4

I see the troops coming, they are on foot. I see them in the aspens on the slope this side of Baptiste Vandale's farm.

I see a pure white horse bearing a rider. The white colour of the horse flashes in the sun. The rider is leaving the road, he wants to get into the open.

I saw a big grass snake striking at the stake.

May 5

My wife encompasses my life. My nation encompasses my way of life. My army, the army which God has given me, encompasses the life I lead. My family has no other life than mine. The Church follows my example and is good to the same extent that I am good.

These words perfectly express Riel's view of himself as a man without a private life, a completely public man, who lived only for the good of his people. Like all great leaders, he had an extraordinary capacity to identify the interests of his followers with his own aspirations, without worrying about possible discrepancies between the two.

Be careful, watch out. The white man and the Orangeman want to trick you. The trap is wide open. It is set, do not rush into it.

For from another side, I see something stupendous coming: a great blow. Stay back, keep together. Let us be ready.

May 6

I see the white man with his battle helmet. The white man is tall. He sees far enough, but his steps do not take him very far, they lead him behind. The white man stumbles; his two feet slowly slide to the wrong side. He cannot stand up; he is effaced little by little; he gradually disappears; he vanishes — because his heart only has room for evil. To be more precise, he has no heart. When I speak of white men, I do not mean brown men.

Here I am, squarely arrived at the time God has marked in the order of things to come. With my own eyes, I saw all the signs of the times which were shown us before now. I did not want to believe that they were really signs of the times. But finally I had to recognize what they were. Yes, before me lies the time identified in many ways, the time announced with all the signs that are supposed to accompany it, as we are told in the Scriptures.

Boue-Chaire-Vile, previously such a fine place, is abandoned! The once fair city of Boue-Chaire-Vile now has no one to protect it. I am calling for help. I would like to wake those who sleep in the profound slumber of sin. They do not hear me, they do not listen to me, they do not obey me. The enemy is coming up the river, he is arriving, he is going to bombard the city. How is it going to resist? No one takes its interests to heart. It is going to fall into the hands of the conqueror. For, having first abandoned God, it is now abandoned by God. It is done. Oh, how many times will you come true, O prophecy? Oh, how many times each century! Oh, how many times each generation?

This is one of Riel's more ambiguous lucubrations. Boue-Chaire-Vile is a sequence of three French words meaning "mud," "flesh" and "vile" — thus suggesting a city sunk in vice and degradation. Also, it is apparently a pun on the name of the town of Boucherville, Quebec, where the ancestral estate of the Taché family was located. Since he was now openly estranged from the Roman Church, Riel presumably had no special regard for Taché and did not mind referring to his birthplace in such a demeaning way. But the context contains no further reference to Taché, but rather suggests that Boue-Chaire-Vile is a symbol of the besieged village of Batoche, now "abandoned by God" for "having abandoned God." I am unable to tie these various threads of meaning securely together, and perhaps the paragraph does not have a single, consistent interpretation. Riel often seems to have punned simply from delight in playing with words, without worrying overmuch about the precise implications of the pun.

The Spirit of God has made me see that my prayers and obeisances are good, that they are pleasing to Him. But the government is harming me; the government's army is waging war upon me. And yet, however harmful that obstacle may have been to me, I am surprised at how easily I have removed it from my path. Anyone who wanted to stop me from praying has been put in his place. When you have confidence in God and Jesus Christ, nothing is difficult any more.

The Spirit of God made me realize the extent of the rights which the Indian possesses to the land of the North-West. Yes, the extent of the Indian rights, the importance of the Indian cause are far above all other interests. People say the native stands on the edge of a chasm. It is not he who stands on the edge of a chasm; his claims are not false. They are just. The land question will soon be resolved, as it must, to his complete satisfaction. Every step the Indian takes is based upon a profound sense of fairness.

May 7

The Spirit of God has inspired me to compose the following prayer: "Let men hear the heavenly voice of Your Spirit telling them about my mission just as Your light showed the Hebrews the divine task of Moses."

Riel thought of himself as leading the Métis, the new chosen people, to their glory, just as Moses had taken the first chosen people to the promised land.

Blessed Virgin Mary! Pray for me to Jesus Christ to please forgive my sins, to please mercifully support my strenuous labours for the success, the victory and the triumph of the cause of religion in the world.

2:15 P.M.

I see the redcoats very close to us. I walked ten feet from their guns, but they didn't do me any harm. They were stunned, and so was I, almost as much. It was not my guards [who protected me.] For there I realized that our men were only little boys and their wives were little girls, fit only to play games together. They were faced with real soldiers. God alone has saved us.

Lépine's ferry is in bad shape. The boat is half full of water. It is drifting loose. Lépine is so careless that he did not even bother to tie up the boat. Here is what my God reveals to me about the future: Oh, whoever you may be, be careful. Never get involved in a Métis war without the help of God. For only God can extract you from the perils of such an enterprise.

May 8

O my God! What must I do to appease Your justice? If You will, please protect me from death, wounds and injuries of any kind, I beg You, for the love of Jesus Christ our Lord, in consideration of Mary Immaculate, Saint Joseph and Saint John the Baptist. In Your great mercy, ward off from me all kinds of sin, death, wounds and any injury. O Immaculate Mary, hear my prayer, I beseech You.

I will have pity on the poor wounded, I will treat the dead with charity, through the grace of Jesus Christ my Saviour and Redeemer. For myself I ask the same graces that I beg You to grant to all my friends.

Oh, I see the state I would be in after the battle if God had not taken pity on me. God has shown me that if He had not saved me in His paternal way, I would be dying, expiring as my strength failed, surrendering my soul and vanishing into the shadows and sadness of death. Oh, thank You my God, for having saved my life in the two battles we have had. Oh thank You, I owe You a thousand million thanks.

Oh, You have showed me, now that the battle is finished and You have carried off the victory, that if You had not protected me mercifully, lovingly, tenderly, I would be overthrown, counted among the dying, hardly able to open my mouth, hardly strong enough to part my lips to receive a little spoonful of ice water in hopes of quenching my thirst and lowering my fever a little. Oh thank You, Jesus Christ! Yes, You are my Saviour! My great and holy Redeemer, glory to You! Glory to Your Almighty and merciful Father. Oh my God, I love You. Thank You for having filled me with good desires and for having led me along the paths of prayer. You have let Your heart be softened by my prayers, and You have deigned to hurl upon our wicked enemies the death, wounds and injuries with which they were threatening me so horribly.

Oh, a hundred thousand million thanks are due to You, O my God, throughout the ages, because You are merciful towards me, towards my wife, my children, my relatives, towards all my enemies. O my God, find a way to be good to our enemies, while still giving us Your successes, Your victories and Your triumphs, for ever and ever.

O my God! Probably it is my sins which made You intend me to be wounded. Oh, give me the most perfect repentance so that, driving all black thoughts from my mind, I may be worthy, through the grace of Jesus Christ, that the battle turn out well for me, without accidents, without wounds, without receiving even the slightest injury. Oh, please efface all my sins; and then I will be confident and truly hopeful that I will not be wounded, that I will not receive any wound, because that will not be in Your intentions.

Great thanks to You, O Jesus, O Mary, O Saint Joseph!

May 8, four in the afternoon

The Spirit of God made me see how arrogant England is, and how she behaves when she does not want to accede to a request. She does everything possible to assure victory over those she does not like; and when she has the upper hand, she cries out in rage, "No, I won't do it."

O my God! Do not let England get the better of me. For she would annihilate me together with my nation. Save me from her power, for the sake of Your Son, for the sake of the glorious Virgin Mary, for the sake of Saint Joseph. O my God! Hasten to help me. Do not delay. Have the charity to send me Your providential help. Please make it arrive soon. Let us be saved through the sweet effects of Your divine goodness. Oh, do not let my good friends, those of them who are coming in Your name, lose a single quarter of an hour en route. Speed them over the distances as if on wings, so that future generations will conserve their memory and all men will be irrefutably convinced that You never abandon those who have put all their trust in You.

O my God! I beg You for the love of Jesus Christ, of the Blessed Virgin and of Saint Joseph, make Your French-Canadian Métis volunteers vigilant, obedient and ready for whatever happens.

Up to this point, Riel's diary had been kept in consecutive fashion, the entries covering the first fifty-seven pages of his notebook. Now, in the midst of the battle of Batoche, he skipped more than two hundred blank pages and made a few entries at the back in pencil.

May 9

The Spirit of God made me see two Métis, two dark men. They were about to be shot dead in the battle, but God has allowed Himself to be moved by fasting and prayer. They were only wounded.

I saw the purple biretta; it disappeared.

I saw the purple surplice disappear; it took some time to fade away.

I saw the purple robe of the postulant nuns disappear.

The biretta, surplice and robe are ecclesiastical vestments used in Roman Catholic ceremonies. Purple, of course, is the colour of power and pomp. Riel's vision seems to say that the power of the Roman Catholic Church will disappear along with its rituals.

May 10

The Spirit of God has instructed me. Here is what He made me announce about those who fight in battle without being properly stationed and without watching the enemy soldiers, for fear of being killed or wounded.

You have closed my eyes so they will not need to see . . . .
The text breaks off due to a torn page.

O my God! Help me, guide me most charitably to place our men well and look after them well, without needlessly exposing myself but also without pusillanimous cowardice. Oh, please support me, so that in the hands of Your Providence I may be as tranquil and calm as a baby in its mother's womb. Open my eyes, give me the greatest trust in You, so that in perfect reliance on Your Omnipotence and infinite goodness, I may be relieved from worry. O my God, I beg You, through Jesus, Mary, Joseph and Saint John the Baptist, grant me Your Holy

Spirit of foresight, of prudence, Your Holy Spirit of courage, Your Holy Spirit of strength and good counsel, for ever and ever, so that we may successfully complete all our good works and have the happiness of performing Your holy will in every respect.

5 Surrender
May 16-24, 1885

The military resistance of the rebels at Batoche was broken on May 12, 1885. For three days, Riel hid in the wooded coulees. Then he surrendered on May 15, after an exchange of notes with General Middleton. Under close guard, he was transported to prison. Initially he was to be sent to Winnipeg, but the federal government quickly realized that Regina was, from their point of view, a preferable place to stage the trial. The destination was changed en route by telegraphic orders, and Riel arrived in Regina on May 23, where he was placed in solitary confinement in the NWMP stockade.

During the trip, Riel made the following entries in his diary. [3] Brief as they are, they are of considerable interest; for they afford an insight into his thinking after the debacle of Batoche. Curiously, there is no direct reference to these dramatic events; Riel seems to want to forget the whole thing. Obviously, he is emotionally exhausted: "the chalice of my spirit is drained." His mood is now one of total submission to the will of God, of renunciation of the attractions of this world, of preparation for death. "Who am I?" asks Riel; "Who am I to try to direct events?" In these words, he seems to renounce completely (although temporarily) his mystical belief in his mission. These days were Riel's spiritual nadir.

> Prophecies which I am compelled to
> write in this book for lack of time
> and lack of health

These prophecies will be useful to the leaders of Manitoba and to many of the elect in the whole world.

---

3. There is in fact some uncertainty about the dating of these entries. For details, see the Appendix.

Sacred Heart of Jesus, You are the light.

May 16

I must detach myself from everything. The chalice of my spirit is drained. O Mary conceived without sin, pray for me.

The pen slips from my hand!

O my God, it is You who are waiting for me. And I was doing the opposite by waiting for You.

May 17

O Mary! Help me to gather and put to good use even the smallest inspirations of the Holy Spirit.

May 18

Lépine! I know what you can do.

The inhabitants of the capital of Manitoba do not want me!

Why boast? And why say that I have well chosen my time to return to Manitoba?

In a second, a traitor could take my life. And I hear divine mercy chanting my *adjuva me* with infinite sadness and gentleness, saying, "Riel! Thirty years of Purgatory."

May 19

I am finished with the pride of life — fancy clothes, fine carriages, canes, pipes of ... *(incomplete).*

May 20

Why do we have comfortable houses? Our home is not here. O Mary conceived without sin, pray for us.

May 21

At my table, I will only have what is strictly necessary — water or milk to drink, no dessert, no syrup.

I do not even want to sit comfortably. I want to punish myself, mortify myself in everything.

May 22

With the help of God and of Jesus and Mary, I must be meek and humble of heart, whatever it costs.

May 23

Down with beautiful hair and vain hair styles! Pretty heads are full of impure thoughts, they speak them aloud, they commit impure acts in great number.

No more useless words! I want to speak meekly. My thoughts must be charitable.

May 24

> O Saviour mine, through Mary's tears,
> I beg of You to give
> Me help, that I may live
> In grace throughout the years.

I put aside opinions and disputes about the personal worth of the different races of men.

No more laziness, slander, calumny. I must strip myself of all feelings of anger, of all melancholy. I must become a true penitent; a Christian, happy inside; polite and charitable towards others. I must be good in the eyes of Jesus Christ. And through divine mercy, let me die while praying; sustained by my God, let me expire under the protection of Mary, to enter into the joys of the true and eternal life without delay.

O Mary, help of Christians, pray for me! Have pity on me! Save me! Save my friends, by making them understand what you have had the goodness to inspire in my mind and heart.

I do not even want to ask God for physical health any longer, for fear of remaining attached to this transitory blessing. I no longer aspire towards the influence which accompanies wealth or fortune. I am afraid that these things would make me forget my goal: a happy death. I love to work for the welfare of the souls of others! But I am afraid that this work might distract me, and that through my weakness I might expose myself to the prisons of Purgatory. However, I trust in God! What I want is never again to have any will of my own, to be in perfect harmony with God, to await His orders, to obey His wishes. And I do not want to act on my own again. I want to be entirely absorbed in the designs of Providence. Who am I? Who am I to try to direct events? Nothing, that's what I am. Even as I speak I could fall dead, and the only echo of my voice would be the hollow resonance of the tomb. O Mary, continue to help me.

6 Imprisonment
August 1885

On August 1, 1885, Louis Riel was convicted of high treason and sentenced to hang. Until this point he had stoutly maintained his spiritual independence, asserting that he was the "prophet of the New World." But the shock of the condemnation temporarily undermined his resolution; and fear of death made him wish to be part of the Roman Church once more, especially so he could receive the sacraments. On August 5, therefore, he signed an abjuration drawn up by Father Fourmond and Father Cochin. He renounced his "false prophetic mission" as the "first cause of his errors."

In this new mood of submission, he began to keep the diary which is printed in this chapter. In his first sentences he declared his absolute loyalty to the church, represented by Archbishop Taché, and vowed that he would willingly submit his diary to the archbishop's censorship.

Fundamentally, he kept to his promise throughout the month of August. There is nothing in this notebook which smacks of heresy; little is recorded in the form of a revelation. Much of the material consists of prayers and meditations on death, carefully written in an orthodox and edifying manner. There is little of the prophetic spontaneity of expression so prominent in the Batoche diary (chapter 4) or the later diary of October 1885 (chapter 7).

Yet, beneath the surface, one can sense a growing optimism and self-confidence on Riel's part. In the later entries, there is relatively less talk of death and repentance, and much more in the way of comments on politics and expressions of hope for escaping the hangman. This development is even visible in the penmanship. The notebook begins in a rounded, meticulous script like that of a professional clerk; but this gradually gives way to Riel's customary bold, vigorous and free-wheeling hand.

By the end of the month, when the notebook was completely filled, Riel had so recovered his buoyancy that he could go back to the beginning and add a new preface, in which he claimed that the entire book was "inspired." Even though it appeared to be written in "common, ordinary language," God had made him write the whole thing. Riel had returned to normal.

Preface
(added after completion of diary)

Everything written in this book is inspired, but I have expressed it in common, ordinary language.

Divine inspiration made me write this book.

I offer it to God, in the name of Jesus Christ, that He might deign to make it serve His greatest glory, the honour of religion, the brilliant success and triumph of truth, my prompt release under present conditions, my most flourishing prosperity, my greater happiness in this world as well as the next, the salvation of all men of good will and the amelioration of the condition of our enemies.

The diary proper begins here:

Everything I will write in this notebook is subject to the approval of His Excellency Monseigneur Alexandre-Antonin Taché, Archbishop of St. Boniface.

At the outset, I renounce anything in my writings which, in Monseigneur's opinion, deserves condemnation.

Submission and obedience to his authority is an essential condition of the true religion.

Through the divine grace of Jesus Christ, I pray to God to make the wisdom of the Archbishop of St. Boniface renowned and to favour him magnificently in everything.

My God! Dwell in me through the divine grace and virtue of Jesus Christ; keep me continually under the powerful protection of Mary, of Saint Joseph and of my blessed patron saints; bless me again in Your mercy now that I have children. Give me the grace to take good care of them through the unceasing prayer of my mind and heart; help me to make them profit from mortification, to make them grow up through penitence.

The angel who dispenses the joys of eternal life appeared to me. He told me: "Even if you should get sick, sit in a way that will mortify your body; be moderate in eating and drinking."

My God! Open the treasure of Your great ideas to me, through Jesus Christ.

The grandeur of Your designs, the attraction of Your thoughts, can save me.

My God! Help me through Jesus Christ.

My God! Drive my misfortunes far from me, through Jesus Christ.

My God! Through the divine grace and influence of Jesus Christ, let the people's interest and wishes persuade and compel the government to inquire into the reason for the troubles which have just occurred. Help them not to inflict any undeserved punishment; enlighten them and support them so they give each man what belongs to him in justice and truth.

O my God! Through Jesus Christ, obtain for me all the evidence and all the witnesses which are necessary to prove, irrefutably and obviously, that justice is entirely on the side of the Métis and the Indians in the war which just took place; thus they should not be punished but indemnified.

In the margin, Riel later wrote: My God, receive my confession and communion through Jesus Christ under the protection of Mary and Joseph and deign to grant this prayer.

My God! Through Jesus Christ, please let the Crown attorneys be aware of the facts and evidence which they lack, and which they need to plead and win the case of the Métis and Indians of the Saskatchewan.

O my God! Bless the Crown attorneys!

O my God! Bless my good lawyers; bless them greatly. Sustain them through the infinite grace and mercy of Jesus Christ.

O my God! Grant the abundance of Your blessing to Father
J.-V. Fourmond and Father Louis Cochin, both Oblates of
Mary Immaculate. Deign to bless me with them in Your
infinite goodness.

Save my body and my soul, through Jesus Christ.

O my God! Through the divine grace and influence of Jesus
Christ, save me from all the punishment I deserve for my sins;
through Jesus Christ, save me from the ignominious death to
which I am condemned.

In the margin, Riel wrote: My confession, my communion are
for the intention of this prayer.

O my God! Through Jesus Christ, grant me the grace to die
of love for You.

In the margin: My confession, my communion [are] for this
prayer.

O my God! Through Jesus Christ, keep my life, my health,
my freedom and my reputation in Your most merciful care.

O my God! Enter into us through the grace of Jesus Christ;
stay with us; abide in us; direct us completely. Never stop
speaking to my conscience, the conscience of my confessor and
that of my Archbishop, in order to make us progress
continually in the way, the truth and the life — more and more
at each moment.

O my God! Communicate the grandeur of Your intentions to
me, the magnetism of Your thoughts, through Jesus Christ.

O my God! Share with me, through Jesus Christ, the
grandeur of Your intentions, the attraction of Your thoughts.

In the margin: My confession, my communion, for the
intention of this prayer.

O my God! Be with me through Jesus Christ, help me
Yourself to make a most holy and perfect communion.

O my God! Through Jesus, Mary and Joseph, grant me the
favour of preparing myself well for death, of dying a holy and
blessed death and of entering without any delay into the joys of
eternal life, as soon as I have breathed my last.

O my God! Through Jesus Christ, fill me with gentleness
and humility in all things, always and everywhere.

O my God! Through Jesus, Mary and Joseph, grant me the grace to truly profit from the time I have left to live: to prepare myself, each day and each moment, for a good and holy death, as if that day and that moment were the last of my existence on earth.

O my God! Deign to inspire me more and more through Jesus Christ, through the goodness of Mary Immaculate, through the most generous help of Saint Joseph, of Saint Louis, of the holy prophet David, of Saint Margaret, of Saint John, of Saint Mary Angelica, of Saint Julia.

The saints named after Jesus and Mary were the patrons of the Metis nation, Riel himself, his wife Marguerite, his son Jean, his daughter Marie-Angélique and his mother Julie.

O my God! Through Jesus, Mary and Joseph, give me the grace to serve You most humbly, through the submission and perfect obedience of my soul to all Your commands and through the greatest deference to all the admonitions of my spiritual advisor.

O my God! Grant me the grace to approach all men in the right way, so they will be glad to support my good initiatives — we beseech You through Jesus Christ.

O my God! I beg you, through Jesus Christ, take care of my health; grant me many opportunities to save my life; guide me, be with me, through Jesus Christ, so I do not neglect any chance to save my life; keep me Yourself, through the most merciful influence of Jesus Christ, in unvarying calmness: not in apathy or indifference, but in the peace of God and in purest surrender to all the dispositions of His Providence. O Mary conceived without sin, pray for us who have recourse to You! Saint Joseph! Intercede for us at every moment.

O my God! Teach me how to do all my actions, great and small, in a way which will make them entirely pleasing to You: inspire me in everything, always and everywhere, through Jesus Christ, through the Blessed Virgin and through Saint Joseph.

O my God! Through Jesus Christ our Lord, through the Blessed Virgin and through Saint Joseph, grant me the grace to take my food calmly and in a way which will be as pleasing to

You as if I were undertaking a rigorous fast under the guidance of Your Holy Spirit.

O my God! Teach me Yourself how much food I should eat to keep up my strength and to enjoy good health. Enlighten me about these things, through the wisdom and mercy of Jesus Christ.

O my God! Grant me, through Jesus, Mary and Joseph, the grace to pass each of my days and all my moments in the most sincere and fervent devotion.

O my God! Through Jesus, Mary and Joseph, grant me all the gifts and all the fruits of Your Spirit so that I may observe Sunday exactly in accord with Your desires and Your holy will.

Help me, through Jesus Christ, so that Sunday worship refreshes me, restores me and does as much good to my body as to my soul.

Remember that at Batoche Riel had transferred the Sabbath from Sunday to Saturday. His praise of Sunday in this context is an indication of his attempt to be submissive to the rules of the Roman Church.

Penance approved by a priest and blessed by him is much more pleasing to God than if it were done outside the authority of the Church (assuming of course, that one can easily consult that authority because priests are nearby or because it is easy to communicate with them).

This is probably an oblique reference to the practice of lay confession which Riel instituted at Batoche.

O my God! Through the divine influence and power of Jesus Christ, make it clear that all the events of my salvation happen in an eminently logical order and are governed by a comprehensive reason which can only be Yours; that consequently the favours and help of which I am the small and humble recipient are entirely controlled by Your Providence, notwithstanding difficulties and obstacles. O my God! Prove, by displaying the divine power of Jesus Christ, by manifesting the effectiveness of the intercession of Mary Immaculate, by justifying our confidence in Saint Joseph — prove that all human efforts can never succeed in impeding the fulfillment of Your plans; that Your Church rises above all, rises in You, even in the stormiest days; and that no one can block the path of Your chosen ones.

O my God! Display the great love of Your heart for all men. Through Jesus, Mary and Joseph, show us how much You desire the salvation of all, even the salvation of those who would not want to save themselves. Show the truth of Your sacred Scriptures. Humble those who exalt themselves. Exalt those who humble themselves to please You.

O my God! I render you countless thanks, through Jesus, Mary and Joseph, for not leading me into temptation, for delivering me from evil. My God! Lead me not into temptation. O my God! Grant me, through Jesus, Mary and Joseph, temperance in eating and drinking, as well as in all pleasures.

O my God! Through Jesus, Mary and Joseph, grant me politeness, tact and civility so that I always address myself to all men in a way that suits their interests and dispositions; thus not only will they be glad to support me with all their might, but it will be more to their advantage to stand behind me without fail and to favour all my good projects.

My God! Through Jesus, Mary and Joseph, always let me address myself to everyone politely, tactfully and civilly according to their dispositions and interests, and thus readily obtain their most energetic and constant material and moral support in all I do, for Your greater glory, for the honour of religion, for the triumph of truth, for my most flourishing prosperity, for my greater happiness in this world and the next, for the salvation of men of goodwill and for the improvement of the condition of the unfortunate.

In the margin: My God, I offer You my communion, praying You to grant mercifully the prayer written on this page.

O my God! I thank You for having preserved in me through Jesus, Mary and Joseph, the appearance, the flower, the strength, the prestige, the activity of youth, even though I am forty years old.

O God, receive my thanks and gratitude
For all the favours You have done to me.

Not my feet alone, but Your solicitude
Has brought me safe along my life's journey.

My God! Now that I have lived forty full years, let me enjoy the prime of life, through Jesus, Mary and Joseph.

My God! Through Jesus Christ, lend an immense effect to the speeches I made before the court on July 31 and August 1, 1885; and let them work for me in every way. O Mary conceived without sin, beg God to hear mercifully my prayer. O Saint Joseph, intercede with God to set the great majority of people in the country on my side.

In the margin: My confession and my communion [are] for the intention of this prayer.

My God! Through the divine grace and influence of Jesus Christ, lend an immense effect to all my speeches and writings. Inspire my words and all my actions; and, through Jesus, Mary and Joseph, let all my words and actions which are in accord with Your holy Church produce extraordinary and wonderful results of salvation for myself, and for all of Christendom, and for all of Catholicism.

Referring to his abjuration of August 5: My God! I have returned to the holy obedience of the Catholic, Apostolic and Roman Church. I pray You, through Jesus, Mary and Joseph, give me the sincerity, the openness and the prudence which are pleasing to You. To Your care, I confide all my interests and affections, both temporal and eternal. (God takes care of the situation.) The logic of obedience is infinite like the will of God. My God! Through Jesus, Mary and Joseph, take most merciful care of all my temporal and eternal interests.

Preserve my life a long time, O my God, I beseech you, through Jesus Christ our Lord, through the Blessed Virgin Mary, through Saint Joseph.

My God! Pardon me, through Jesus Christ our Lord, for the haste and lack of respectful and devout attention with which I have so often pronounced and written Your holy and adorable name, as well as the names of Jesus, Mary, Joseph and all the saints, especially the names of my venerated patrons Saint Louis and Saint David, and the names of everything sacred.

Remit the punishment due to these faults, through Jesus Christ; do not punish me as I deserve, but grant me mercy through the goodness of Your Son!

In the margin: My God, I offer you my communion, begging you to hear my prayer.

O my God! Through Jesus Christ, make Archbishop Alexandre-Antonin Taché and Bishop Grandin declare themselves in favour of my mission, openly and without reserve. Let them come tell me so in their concern for my temporal and eternal salvation, under the protection of Mary Immaculate and the safeguard of Saint Joseph, our great protector, the chosen patron of the Métis and patron of the universal Church.

My God! Through the divine grace, influence and power of Jesus Christ, every time I am in danger of losing my life, let it be counterbalanced by a great number of occasions and circumstances favourable to the preservation of my existence. Thus may the infinite resources of your Providence continually save me from peril. When I am ceaselessly surrounded and favoured by unprecedented good fortune, make it obvious to men that I am sustained by You alone. For You do what no human power can: to my advantage, You bring together the efforts of the small number of really good people with those of the large number of mediocre men. Nor can any merely human power use for the triumph of the Church such a strange coalition of forces to which many people, even those hostile to our interests, are contributing without realizing it.

In the margin: My God, I offer You my communion, beseeching You to hear my heart's prayer, which You have helped me to formulate on this sheet of paper.

My God! Guide me through Jesus Christ. Through His divine influence, help me to prepare for a death which will be totally pleasing to You. Inspire in me Yourself the meditations which will better lead my Christian and Catholic brothers to prepare themselves well for death. Reveal to me the greatest and most edifying insights on the subject of death. Through the grace of Jesus Christ, let me express them simply, without ostentation. Let me have the signal honour of benefiting my Christian brothers and my Catholic co-religionists.

My God! Create a new and pure intelligence in me. Renew and sanctify my will, my memory and my freedom through Jesus Christ. O Mary conceived without sin, pray for us who have recourse to you. O Saint Joseph, our great protector, chosen patron of the Métis and of the universal Church, have pity on us, have pity on me, intercede for us, obtain for us from God all the graces we need!

In the name of the Father and of the Son and of the Holy Ghost. Amen.

August 11, 1885

Our mind reflects on all subjects, many of which are insignificant. We are careful to arrange a torn garment [so the rip will not show]; we avoid wearing it if we can do without it.

But there is one thing which we struggle to keep out of our mind: the true condition of our soul in the sight of God.

Has evil pierced the chain mail of our moral welfare? We do not hasten with alacrity to find the remedy in God. We remain in our sad state. We even perversely try to make our recklessness a platform to stand on.

We are vigilant, taking precautions in everything which touches our transitory interests on earth. But as for the interests of our immortal soul, we permit ourselves neglect upon neglect, forgetfulness upon forgetfulness.

Neglect becomes so powerful in us that it succeeds in taking over our reason and deadens it. The salutary unease of our conscience disappears in the reign of lethargy.

Forgetfulness of the sad injuries inflicted on our soul and our moral health takes possession of our faculties and makes them torpid. At this point our intelligence is asleep and loses touch with the realities of our future life.

Once that sleep has begun, man is only dreaming of the trivial things of his short temporal life.

He walks, he talks, he moves: but in the sight of God all his activities are no more than wretched sleep-walking.

Death! Among those whom God lets you carry off each day,

how many are not in that condition? Among those you take, how many are on their guard?

Blessed be the judge who told me: "I have set the day of your death. Now you know it, I am warning you: get ready. Use the time I'm giving you."

Blessed be the six jurymen who recommended me to the mercy of the court.

Riel's jury found him guilty of high treason, but also recommended mercy in sentencing. However, under the law, the presiding judge had no choice but to impose capital punishment, a situation which the jury apparently did not understand. Once they convicted Riel, only the Crown could lessen his sentence.

Blessed be the judge who said to me: "If you obtain clemency, I will be the first to rejoice! But prepare yourself."

My God! Through Jesus Christ, through the holy intercession of Mary, under the protective shield of Saint Joseph, inspire me with the most vivid conceptions of death; the most salutary, the most novel reflections; the most original and compelling meditations; the most dreadful thoughts about my last moments; so that I can profit as a Christian from the time I have yet to live.

Death is not a phantom; she is a truth which I will meet and whose force I will feel. She stands ahead of me as certainly as the road on which I set my foot.

Death waits for me as the inkwell waits for my pen, to drench it in dark and sombre tears.

Is my bed as useful to me as my coffin will be? The breathing which relaxes me and which takes place so easily in my heart and breast will stop one day and I will expire. Death, you will conquer me. You will put an end to my physical life. And my soul will be left with the moral life I have made for myself.

Is the idea I have of internal peace correct? If I eat at every meal without ever thinking of mortifying myself; if I always dress in clothes which suit my fancy as much as possible; if my vanity, my self-love have free rein in my conscience; if I almost never pray, or rather if I pray more for appearance's sake than to ask for the blessings of salvation in spirit and in truth — whom do I resemble? What testimony do I bear when I take heaven by storm? The warning that Jesus Christ has given me is very explicit: "From the days of John the Baptist, the Kingdom of Heaven suffers violence."

What violence do I do to myself when I exert myself to procure all imaginable pleasures, when I am selective in my food, when I surround myself with upholstered chairs and velvet sofas, when my bedroom all by itself is a city of Sybaris? Great God! Your Son died on the cross for us, and I die on a hill of pillows, on a mountain of feathers and goose down! Even my casket is a luxurious dwelling place! Pride of Death, can you ever have a more sumptuous throne than the nineteenth century has given you?

Death, where are you leading the children of pride, the idolaters of comfort? I live in comfort, catering to all the whims of my fallen nature. How can I hope that Paradise will open to receive me when I die? Alas! Alas! A man who becomes indebted to others succeeds in paying his debts only in pain and sorrow. Who said that in matters of religion the debtor could go into debt without limit and at the end of his life he would surely be paid back? But paid back with what, if he has done nothing but go into debt?

Blessed is he who faithfully keeps the commandments of God!

Blessed is he who neither blasphemes nor swears!

Blessed is he who does not turn Sunday into a day of idleness or voluptuousness, but observes it as a day of prayer and religious worship!

Blessed are pure minds and bodies! Blessed is he who refuses to participate in injustice!

Blessed is he who agrees to work and accept a wage only after assuring himself of the righteousness and worth of the tasks he is asked to perform!

Blessed is he who brings the spirit of justice to the letter of the law, and who interprets it conscientiously!

Blessed is he who does not abuse his profession!

Blessed is he who does not profane his talents!

Blessed is he who accepts criticism well, and who, having made a mistake, repents voluntarily.

(August)

My God! Through Jesus Christ, vastly extend the effect You have been pleased to give to the speeches which You made me give in court the last day of July and the first of this month. Under the protection of Mary, under the charitable shield of Saint Joseph, display the immense effect of the words and ideas which You inspire in me. Spread it beyond the United States in all countries of the world. Nourish that immense effect. Make it lasting, by arousing the interest of all the chief politicians of the country, through Jesus Christ, whose power and goodness are infinite.

The paragraph breaks off here due to a torn page. In the margin Riel has written: O my God, I offer You my communion, begging You to hear the prayer which echoes in my mind because of You and which I have written on these pages. Through Jesus, Mary and Joseph.

Here follows a fragment of a prayer for persons who cannot be identified: ... may the Good Lord reward you for what you are doing for me. May He grant you a hundred times as much on this earth and a thousand times more in the next life. In your generosity, keep death away from me for many years by combatting those who want to make me die. For my part, I am going to pray to the Good Lord to hear my prayers on your behalf, through Jesus Christ, through the intercession of Mary, through the protection of Saint Joseph. May death stay far from you and come to your bedside only when you expect it, when you are entirely prepared for the encounter. More than that, I am asking God to please send death's visit only when you have already long desired it; when your good and beautiful souls, impatient to taste the joys of heaven, have tamed death and transformed it into joy, deliverance and triumph.

Tremble my heart, and bid my soul resound!

Before you Peace displays a vaster field
Than open countryside or battle ground.
Before God's peace the grave cannot but yield.

Amidst gigantic struggles, peace of mind
Alone outweighs all other qualities.
The man who has it certainly will find
Defeats becoming mighty victories.

I tell you, friends, 'tis only Jesus's peace
Which fills our hearts with joy in every way.
Though good, the blessings of this world soon cease
To satisfy, and lead us far astray.

Have peace of mind, and trust God to uncover
New depths of joyous wisdom in your soul.
With the peace of God, your eyes will soon discover
       Happiness — entire, whole!

To do God's will lends us tranquillity.
It makes us calm when danger comes in view.
Toward heaven lift your hands in humility
Through the grace of God we can be born anew!

Blessed Virgin, send down a flood of light
To illuminate the human race.
A river of prayers I ask through Joseph's might
To save us today, and all our sins efface.

A mouthful too much at our meals can only do us harm. O you who live in comfort, a swallow, a mouthful less at your feasts can only do you good.

Death has many kinds of claims on me. When I am hungry, it is death subtly reminding me of my weakness and coyly threatening to carry me off if I do not fortify myself against her by taking nourishment. Again, each time that sleep overcomes me, it is death warning me of extinction. If I do not rest, she is only too ready to push matters to a conclusion and rob me of the charms and pleasures of life.

I come close to a roaring fire to warm myself. My sense of well-being changes to discomfort. I begin to feel too hot. What is it? It is death telling me: "I would like you to stay there; it wouldn't take me long to get you then."

I am out in the cold; I am doing all I can to protect myself. I must get to my destination. I am forced to struggle against the weather, which numbs me. It is death who is at my side, consoling herself for not having yet gotten me, for she sees how hard it is for me to escape her. She is trifling with me. Over and over she tells me to watch out. She does not conceal the fact that she follows me day and night. There is no chance that she will slip and miss her mark when she tells me to pay attention. For she is sure of me. While I tremble and barely succeed in keeping from her the slender thread of my life, which she is always on the verge of cutting, death hideously smiles at me. My fear is her amusement. Death is playing with me. She is certain to put her hand on me, just as the grown-up is sure of catching the child with whom he has agreed to play tag for a moment's fun.

Death lies beside me in my bed. When sleep begins to close my eyes, she whispers. Her voice touches the bottom of my heart; it says that sleep is a rehearsal for death. "Notice," she says, "how sleep comes to you. That is almost how I will greet you on the day you will have to meet me. I will close your eyes as sleep does. I will take possession of you in the same way that repose creeps over your senses. And I will let you wake up, but not in this world. For when we meet, it will only be to introduce you to the things of eternity."

Death reveals how much [she] is attached to me. She speaks affectionately, saying: "I am your wife. I don't want to turn my back on you. You'll never hear me say I'm leaving you. I follow faithfully wherever you go. I am always trying to embrace you, for I love you. I am bored when I'm away from you. My only desire is to have and possess you. When you feel indisposed or sick, don't forget that I am near you and want to abide with you. A moment will come when I will take you. Your last breath will be the sign of my union with you. And when everyone, even your relatives and friends, has fled from you and deserted the place where you have been put, I, Death, whom you don't love and whom you fear so much, I will still be your constant companion. Who can separate me from you? Who will come to take you from my arms? Who will disturb our union, when I press you to my breast in the grave?"

O my God! How has Death become my fiancée, with all the horror I feel towards her? And how can it be that the more she repels me, the more she seeks me out?

Death, the Son of God has triumphed over your cruelties. Your torments are not what they used to be. Since Jesus Christ has made you more gentle, there is less grief in seeing you arrive.

It is not you I fear as much as the judgment which follows you. I want to be reconciled with you. Death, I want to make you into a good death. Through the divine grace, influence, power and mercy of Jesus Christ, through the goodness of Mary Immaculate, through the charity of Saint Joseph, I agree to marry you before the Church, on the condition that our wedding is one of light and eternal rest, amid the joys of Paradise!

August 13, 1885

My God! Through the divine grace, influence, power and mercy of Jesus Christ, inspire Your pious bishops and devoted priests with renewed ardour and zeal for the movement which You are promoting through my inspired words and actions. My God, do not let Your clergy take me for a man without conviction. Make them aware of all my actions and motives so that they see me above all as an obedient man, through Jesus Christ. O Mary conceived without sin, O Saint Joseph, my great protector, chosen patron of the Métis, patron of the universal Church! Intercede for me! Pray for me! Protect us, guide us.

My God! In Your compassion, through Jesus Christ, let me make a favourable impression upon public opinion in all respects, as a gentleman, a scholar, a true Christian and a good Catholic.

My God! Hasten to make everyone see, through the almighty grace of Jesus Christ, that You have sent me to redeem the honour of Your people, with the grace of the prayers of Mary Immaculate, as well as to redeem the glory of the true faith, through the influence which Saint Joseph enjoys with You.

My God! Hasten to make the people understand, by the gracious inspiration of Jesus Christ, that the surest way for me to procure the maximum glory for You, to honour religion most effectively, to edify my neighbour more, and to attain the first and highest degree of perfection is to keep myself in complete rapport with the holy Catholic Church. Please do not delay in making that apparent to all men of good will and even to those who have only some slight inclination to do good. I beg You through Jesus Christ. O Mary conceived without sin, pray for us who have recourse to you. O Saint Joseph, intercede for us who rely on you.

In the margin: O my God! Govern me Yourself. Accept my communion, hear my prayer.

My God, through Jesus Christ, through the merciful power of Jesus Christ, make all those who drink champagne and intoxicating liquor support me. All those who frequent restaurants — inspire them to support my words and actions. Let them be converted by helping me, and let them help me by being converted! O Mary conceived without sin, pray for us! O Saint Joseph, intercede for us. Jesus, save me. Mary, protect me. Saint Joseph, watch over me.

August 14, 1885

My God, give me all those intentions that will help save my life, through Jesus Christ.

My God, through the grace of Jesus Christ, produce in me the most resolute intention to obtain grace and preserve my life.

My God, take away from me, through Jesus Christ, any disposition which tends to put me in danger of death.

Because I have so much confidence in You, my God, hear

my humble prayers. Through Mary Immaculate, through Saint Joseph, at the feet of Jesus Christ, I address to You the supplications with which my heart overflows. Do not let me commit one of those imprudent, miscalculated acts whose effect would be to cause my death. Guide me, be with me, O my God, sustain me, through Jesus, Mary and Joseph. Let me be in perfect harmony with the Archbishop of St. Boniface and the experienced, charitable and devoted confessor whom he has had the goodness to send me.[4] Transform us entirely from this day forth.

My God! Through Jesus Christ, send men to my aid who are learned, able, respectful, serious, worthy, influential and powerful, in order to give the authorities a clear and satisfactory solution to all the complexities, all the irregularities, all the illegalities, all the unconstitutionalities and all the sophisms which have been heaped on me in order to destroy me.

In the margin: O my God, receive my communion, mercifully grant my prayer.

Mary! You are powerful before God; pray, intercede for me unceasingly. Persuade Jesus Christ Himself to help me.

Saint Joseph! Our great protector, chosen patron of the Métis, patron of the universal Church, obtain grace and mercy for me.

My God! Through Jesus Christ, inspire all public figures and newspapers to reproduce my ideas accurately, to explain them reasonably, to report their authority and true significance and to use their power well. My God! Through the divine power and mercy of Jesus Christ, display the views which I am expressing in Your name and on Your behalf. Through the intercession of Mary Immaculate, let everyone without exception study their import and embrace them eagerly.

My God! Through the most loving intervention of Jesus Christ, lend enormous popularity to the interesting thoughts which You deign to make me announce under the protection of Saint Joseph.

My God! Through the goodness of Jesus Christ, bless me

4. That is, Father André.

along with my wife, my children, my gentle and beloved mother, my brothers and sisters, my brothers- and sisters-in-law; bless me, through the Blessed Virgin Mary, with my beloved father-in-law, my mother-in-law and all the relatives of my wife. Bless me, through Saint Joseph, with all my relatives, friends and benefactors; and in general with all those who are dear to me. Bless me, through the gentleness and humility of Jesus, Mary and Joseph, with all my enemies, even the ones who are most hostile to me. May Your inexhaustible benedictions suffuse me in all things, always and everywhere, with Archbishop Alexandre-Antonin Taché, with the curé Joseph-Noël Ritchot, with the priest Jean-Baptiste Primeau, with the Jesuit Frederick Eberschweiler, with the Oblate Father Alexis André, my spiritual director, with all the episcopacy and all the Catholic clergy of the whole world. May Your ineffable benedictions unite me most intimately with all Your elect, by ceaselessly impelling all good men, all classes of society to become daily more enthused about my projects. And may the influence of Your Holy Spirit, which nothing can withstand, renew the face of the earth.

In the margin: O my God! Help me to identify myself with You in Holy Communion. I offer You my reception of the Holy Eucharist today. Charitably grant the prayer written on these pages.

My God! Lead me, through the grace of Jesus Christ, in the most perfect obedience. Be pleased with my submission. Apply the infinite merits of our Lord Jesus Christ to my obedience.

My God! Support me through the divine charity of Your eternal Son; with the protection of Mary, His Mother; under the care of Saint Joseph, His guardian and foster father. Let the renunciation of my own will and the identification of my liberty with that of the priest, my spiritual director, obtain from Your infinite mercy more grace, favour, generosity and precious blessings than would be obtained by the most rigorous fast and the greatest mortifications undertaken on my own initiative, outside the blessed direction of the priest who guides me.

In the margin: My confession, my communion are for the intention of this prayer.

My God! Through Jesus Christ, help me develop the habit

of each day preparing myself courageously for death.

My God! Through the divine grace and influence of Jesus Christ, give me all good habits. According to the multitude of Your mercies, through the prayers of the most holy Virgin Mary and of the powerful Saint Joseph, make me develop the habit now of preparing myself well for death, so that nothing ever distracts me from this pious exercise. Inculcate in me the heavenly principle of seriously preparing myself each day for a happy death. Do not let that preparation be superficial, but profoundly rooted in the depths of my soul.

My God! Through Jesus Christ, through Mary Immaculate, through Saint Joseph, place me Yourself in a state of unshakeable calmness, so that even the noisy and distracting affairs of the world never divert me from salutary thoughts of death, or of You!

My God! Open to me through Jesus Christ the sanctuary of the most heavenly meditations about death, judgment, Paradise and the punishments of the other world.

Open to me the treasure of Your great ideas, through Jesus Christ.

Meditation on Death

According to the death sentence handed down against me by the court, I have no more than thirty-four days to live. These thirty-four days seems as fleeting to me as thirty-four hours.

They disappear more quickly than the Montana snow under the voracious southwest wind, the hot breath of the chinook.

There will come a moment when I will have only thirty-four hours to live. O my God, help me through the mercy of Jesus Christ to take advantage of every second of my existence.

O Lord Jesus! Be moved by the intercession of Mary. Help me to make myself holy enough to appear before You. Let me arrive in peace at the end of my career, protected by the charity of Saint Joseph all the days of my life. Let death find me ready and totally absorbed in thoughts of You!

There will come a moment when I will have only thirty-four seconds to live.

O merciful and most holy Redeemer of the world, surround me then with Your infinite clemency! Full of confidence, filled with devotion to Saint Joseph, may I surrender my soul to you as calmly and peacefully as possible, in the midst of the perfect graces of redemption.

August 15, 1885

My God! Grant me, through Jesus Christ, the grace to receive all my rebukes humbly and to use them for my greater spiritual and material benefit.

My God! Deliver me, through Jesus Christ, deliver me from the evil sensations and convulsions to which our bodies are exposed during our nightly sleep. Through the powerful protection of Mary, drive far away from my repose the nightmares, phantoms and empty images to which our spirits are sometimes exposed while we sleep.

My God! Through the total power of Jesus Christ, prevent Your holy priests from ever becoming lukewarm in Your service. Never let them give up promoting the interests of Your glory and of religion, as well as the salvation of souls! My God, reanimate the virtue of their apostolic and edifying zeal, through Jesus Christ. Through the protection of Mary and the intercession of Saint Joseph, unite me more closely than ever to the virtuous curé Joseph-N. Ritchot. Bring me close to him, and him to me, through the effect of the divine graces of Jesus Christ, so that we constitute one heart and one soul, under the direction of Archbishop Alexandre-A. Taché — for Your greater glory, for the honour of religion, for the triumph of truth, for our greater happiness in this world and the next, for the salvation of men of good will and for the improvement of the condition of our enemies.

Saint Joseph, intercede for me with Mary! Holy Virgin Immaculate, intercede for me with Jesus Christ. Lord Jesus, my lovable Saviour, I humbly ask in Your name that You spare me from the punishment to which I am unfortunately condemned. Spread the wings of Your mercy above me so that I surrender my soul in a burst of love for You, instead of dying strangled by the rope. Protect me with the shield of Your kindness so that I may die from a holy rapture of divine love, instead of ending my life on the scaffold. Do not let me die with my mouth gaping open from the shock of the drop; but let it stay open a little after having received the Holy Eucharist, having sung Your praises and having rendered You countless acts of thanksgiving.

My God, if You want my tongue to stick out between my lips, in honour of Holy Communion, let it happen through Jesus, Mary and Joseph, thanks to my fortunate practice of receiving You in the blessed Host. Save me from the rope and its ugly effects. My tongue goes by itself, under the strong impulse of Your spirit, toward the bread, toward the essential food and active medicine of Your Holy Table. Do not use the rope to draw me up to heaven. The attraction of Your love is great enough to carry me to You.

Jesus, who deigned to endure all the cruelties and ignominies of death, spare me please from the agony to which I am condemned. Be my refuge and my redeemer. You are my merciful Saviour. O Jesus, Mary and Joseph! Shield and protect me from any kind of death which is accompanied by the gnashing of teeth.

My God! Sustain the zeal, fervour and spirit of truth in Your bishops and priests, that they may forever keep religion in the ascendant, through Jesus Christ.

Meditation on Judgment

The sayings of Jesus Christ, which He has left for me to study in the Gospel, will judge me on the last day.

If I have done my best, if I have tried to follow the words of Christ, my spirit will bear witness. Not only will I have confidence in God because He is infinitely good, but the virtue of hope will be present in me. It will strengthen me by making me realize that the peace I will enjoy after death will be a result of the good will I have exhibited.

If, aided by divine goodness, I have been faithful to the command to give alms, I will commend myself to the Saviour, with at least some confidence in my respectful and religious expectation that His charitable hand will open the gates of Paradise for me.

If I faithfully submit to the authority of the priest, never forgetting that sins taken away by him on earth are taken away at the same time in heaven by the grace of God; if I commend myself well to our Lord, expressing my trust in Him like the good thief on the cross; if my religious sentiments genuinely accept the priest as the minister or representative of Jesus Christ, then all my actions are founded on redemption, and my death is only the last step of my complete reconciliation with the divine essence. All the judgments of my spirit are judgments of consolation. Some rest purely on faith while others rest on established grounds of hope; some are established on love and others, in the last analysis, are based on the foundations of sincere contrition. Thus my soul obtains peace, through the Holy Spirit.

My God, shower Archbishop Alexandre-Antonin Taché with Your most admirable gifts. Kindle the light of the most extraordinary genius in him, in virtue of the merits of Jesus Christ and for the sake of Mary Immaculate and Saint Joseph.

My God! Through the grace and power of Jesus Christ, favour the steadfast and judicious cure of St. Norbert, Father Joseph-N. Ritchot. Guide him in the path of Your sublime plans. Exalt him; make him fall in love with the grandeur of Your works. Let his humble spirit soar to the heights of heaven. O Mary, O Joseph, pray for the curé J.-N. Ritchot.

My God! Through the divine influence of Jesus Christ, inspire the charitable Father Alexis Andre, my spiritual director. Give him the abundance of Your Spirit. Bless his frankness. Let his candour shine like the marvelous disk of the moon when it emerges from dense clouds and launches itself into the midst of the clear blue sky. Under the protection of Mary Immaculate, let his letters become solemn proclamations of political truths. Let him enlighten not only the Dominion of Canada but also the United States; and let the echoes of public opinion repeat them across the ocean in France and in all countries where French is spoken.

Let his writings become popular and be translated into different languages, for the greater glory of God, for the edification of my neighbour and for my greater happiness in this world and the next. And ensure that, after having served You well during a long life, he dies under the protection of Jesus, Mary and Joseph, to enter without delay into eternal joy.

August 16, 1885.
Celebration of the Assumption
of Blessed Mary ever Virgin

My God! Through Jesus Christ our Lord, give me the grace to love prayers, exercises of piety, the priest's instructions — and above all Holy Communion, incomparably more than any material food, even the most delectable dishes. Under the protection of Mary Immaculate and under the protection of Saint Joseph, let the hours of devotion, when they arrive, cause me more joy than the dinner hour.

You have given me a new heart by adoring You in the Blessed Sacrament.

Blessed Virgin Mary, glorious queen of the Assumption, pray for me, pray for us, that our coffins[5] be filled with charity, obedience, humility and justice. Thus belonging more to heaven than to earth, let them rise like Yours, unimpeded, up to the eternal home of Paradise!

Blessed Virgin, merciful Mother of the Assumption, I obey: teach me yourself, at the feet of Jesus, to obey perfectly. Persuade the Good Lord to heal all my spiritual and physical maladies, for the sake of Jesus Christ our Lord and through the prayer of Your chosen and worthy servant, Alexandre-Antonin

5. A pun. Instead of "cercueils" (coffins), Riel wrote "Serre-cueilles," literally "grip-harvests." The idea implied is that death is like the harvest at which the fruits of our lives are gathered up.

Taché, and through the blessing of the charitable Father André, my spiritual director.

I think that today half of Lower Canada is in favour of the movement, thanks to Jesus, thanks to Mary, thanks to Saint Joseph.

I have many forebodings, I feel them, they are very clear, that the federal ministers from Lower Canada are going to be in a bad way. Unless I am mistaken, they are already in trouble and Sir John is beginning to worry.

The powerful men who have tried to discredit Mgr. Taché, Father Ritchot and the clergy are in turn being discredited now. Their recklessness towards the interests of this country is going to be reflected in the number of seats they occupy in the House and in the Government. The complaints and the good suggestions of the holy Bishop of St. Albert,[6] the importunate letters òf many members of his pious clergy have not been forgotten. Providence has kept track of them and epitomized them in the battles in Saskatchewan. That is what I am sure of. And the current situation seems to me to be guided by the express permission of God, so that everything that Mgr. Taché, Father Ritchot, Mgr. Grandin, the clergy of Manitoba and of the North-West have written and done for fifteen years in the interest of this vast land, which they understand so well, will prevail at the right time.

Perhaps the Conservatives will only be able to maintain themselves in Ottawa by turning the entire situation of the last fifteen years against the honourable gentlemen Blake and Mackenzie! Furthermore, it seems to me to lie in the well-laid plans of God that, to remain in power, they will have to honour the clergy twice as much to atone for the way their lack of energy and good faith has allowed the clergy to be vilified by their opponents.

There are two circumstances which to me seem providentially brought together for the coming triumph of the Church in the Anglo-Saxon countries:

1. the Conservatives are in power in England, the United

6. Bishop Grandin.

States[7] and the Dominion of Canada.

2. the Liberals are organized and powerful, and in the United States have the additional prestige of having liberated four million men.[8] In England they have carried out great reforms under the leadership of Gladstone; and in the Dominion of Canada they have the advantage of having joined hands with a movement which, thank God, is growing in popularity not only every day but every second.

England, Canada and the United States are three closely related countries. In each place, public opinion discusses questions in terms which are understood in the others; so the trend of ideas leads the people to conclusions which, once adopted in one of these countries, will not take long to become acceptable in the other two.

As far as the specific, contemporary situation in Canada is concerned, the episcopacy and the clergy and, as luck would have it, Archbishop Taché, Bishop Grandin and their priests seem to me to be in an especially favourable position for getting results.

Let the Conservatives, God willing, continue to be pressed by an opposition which is rapidly gathering strength. Then their only chance of salvation will be to return to the influence of the clergy.

The grace of Jesus Christ, coming to the aid of experience and wisdom, will bring out of current events enormous consequences for the glory of God, for the honour of religion, for the triumph of truth, for our greater good in this world and the next, for the benefit of good men and for the improvement of the condition of the indifferent and of our opponents.

Meditation — August 17, 1885

The dinner hour is a time of day which I enjoy. What makes me

---

7. Riel called the American political parties by Anglo-Canadian names. The Democrats were "Conservatives," the Republicans "Liberals."
8. The emancipation of the Negro slaves.

like to eat is the good taste of the food. That is how I keep up my strength. The satisfaction of having a full stomach is another substantial pleasure that it is impossible to be indifferent to. Thus it is in the nature of things that I should enjoy my meals.

But if the nourishment of the body is enjoyable, that of the spirit should be more so; for to the extent that the spirit is much more excellent than the body, that which strengthens the former should be superior in nature to that which serves to feed the latter.

Prayer attracts the divine spirit to visit the human soul and settle there; thus the effect of prayer is to nourish me spiritually. Pious and prescribed reflections produce results of the same type. Good works based on motives of true religion, spiritual communion, reception of the sacrament of the Eucharist, accompanied by a disposition conforming to the wishes of Jesus Christ, are sources of reliable sustenance most precious for my spirit. How does it happen then that I do not like these acts of devotion as much as the act of my physical nourishment? The reason seems very simple. I accomplish these [spiritual] works in such a defective way that I hardly get any benefit from them. Because I am missing the effects, I am also missing the attractiveness.

My God, support me, through Jesus Christ our Lord, that I may pray, think, reflect, understand, speak, act, write and serve You in everything, always and everywhere, so as to draw You more and more into myself. May Your divine gifts and fruits continually nourish me and ever increase my powers, with the result that I experience during my exercises of piety even greater pleasure than I get from eating the food which my body needs to maintain its strength and health.

O Mary, wonderful Mother of the Assumption, intercede for me that it may be thus! O Saint Joseph! O my great protector! O chosen patron of the Métis! Patron of the universal Church, pray to God for me, for my wife and children, for my mother, my father-in-law, my brothers and sisters, my brothers- and sisters-in-law, for my cousins, nephews and nieces, uncles and aunts, for my relatives and neighbours, my benefactors and friends; for the vicar of Jesus Christ on earth, for all bishops and ordained priests; especially for all persons, ecclesiastics and laymen, who have done so much for us and who are still assisting us before God and men. Pray for all of us. Obtain for us from Jesus the grace to find and recognize that the true practice of religion is that spiritual nourishment which, by being copious and abundant enough, becomes most attractive; and which, by harmonizing us with the divine essence, elevates our strength to eternal life.

Meditation on Judgment

Divine grace of Jesus Christ, cleanse my conscience so well that nothing remains in its memories except whatever is entirely immersed in faith, hope and charity as well as perfect contrition. O Jesus Christ, Son of the living God, absorb me completely in the bosom of Your mercy. In Your great love, let me join You in Paradise on the very day of my last breath.

Do not judge me according to my merits but according to Your infinite love. Surround me with the reward of Your passion. Pay my ransom to the Good Lord our Father, by offering him the treasure of Your goodness and the sum of Your sufferings. Redeem me, for You are the only Saviour, the unique Redeemer of men.

Lamb of God, take away my sins from first to last. Take away the punishment due to my sins.

Lamb of God, take away all my faults, from first to last; take away all the consequences of my faults.

Lamb of God, take away all my offences, from first to last, from greatest to least. Take away all the results of my offences.

Lamb of God, who take away the sins of the world, take away the sins of all men of good will.

Lamb of God, who take away the sins of the world, take away the sins of all those who have some inclination to do good.

Lamb of God, who take away the sins of the world, take away the sins of all my enemies.

My God, judge me, through Jesus Christ, according to the

infinite kindness of Your Spirit, following the ineffable mercy of Your paternal heart.

Meditation on the Influence which the Sins of Parents Exercise on Children!

I have passed on my propensities to my children. I have communicated to them the tendencies I had towards both good and evil. O my God, which of these two inclinations is stronger? O my little children, are you heirs of more good than evil through me? Or have you received from me more tendencies to do evil than to do good?

Mystery of anxiety! I am meditating on you in order to commend myself and my children to Almighty God. What is impossible in the sight of men is possible in the sight of God! O my God, even if I have regrettably communicated to my children a greater tendency toward evil than toward good, I commend them to You. And because You are infinite in power and kindness, I beg You to save them through the grace of Jesus Christ, under the protection of Mary, under the protection of Saint Joseph.

Redemption is a mystery. That is, the salvation of men often takes place in a most incomprehensible way, if one considers the obstacles and difficulties with which the way to heaven is hedged about, especially for certain souls.

I am taking the initiative by making this present meditation. How many people have lived badly all the days of their lives! They have raised and have even conceived their children in the midst of the greatest iniquities. To them I point out the path of consolation, hope and trust, so that they may, with the help of God, attain peace on their last day, rendering glory to the Son of God, Jesus Christ our Lord, who offers a wondrous redemption.

Let us ask Him anything, whatever it may be, so that He may grant it, according to the most loving invitation which He Himself has left us in the Gospel! Let us ask Him for our salvation and that of our children! And He will grant it to us and our children.

The sincerity of prayer is demonstrated by fasting, obedience, almsgiving and other mortifications.

Lamb of God, who take away the sins of the world, take away the evil or the roots of sin which are present in the hearts of our children.

Lamb of God, in place of the weakness which exists in the hearts of our children, give strength and gifts and the fruits of Your Holy Spirit.

My God! Through the grace, influence, power and mercy of Jesus Christ, let Gabriel Dumont's motives and point of view coincide with those of the clergy of Montana, Dakota and Minnesota. Blessed Virgin Mary, Saint Joseph, beseech God and petition our Lord that perfect harmony may exist between Gabriel Dumont and the clergy.

May Gabriel Dumont be an instrument of peace and clemency for the North-West and for me. O my God, hear my prayer for the sake of Jesus, Mary and Joseph.

August 18, 1885

I am very confident that today the Good Lord is annulling the sentence of death passed against me.

But if people's minds remain as upset as they are now, I will need to be cautious.

My God! Who is it who scatters the clouds after the storm, if not You? Set the serenity of heaven above my head, O God thrice good. Give me calm and peace through Jesus Christ. You can do it easily, although it appears very difficult. The omnipotence of Your Spirit knows no obstacles, since Your infinitely loving Son returned to You and since He intercedes in our favour before the throne of Your mercy. Blessed Virgin Mary, whose glory shines without stain and whose birth was so beautiful! Saint Joseph, our great protector, chosen patron of the Métis, patron of the universal Church, make the storms disappear which roar and thunder above me. Make it clear as far as my eye can see. Please open to me an entirely new career, more peaceful and more beautiful than men would ever be able to imagine.

My God! Grant me, through Jesus, Mary and Joseph, the true feelings of compunction which I need to prepare for a good death, in a most Christian fashion.

O March 19, may you ever be blessed among the Métis and the servants of Saint Joseph.

O July 24, may you ever be blessed in my family, among my relatives, in my nation and in the whole Church, by all the servants of Saint Joseph.

O September 24, may you ever be blessed and fittingly observed, because you are the day of our Lady of Mercy!

May you ever be observed among the Métis because their first national celebration of the feast of Saint Joseph took place under your favouring sun, and because all Saskatchewan trembled with joy, when dawn broke over it in 1884!

These dates require some explanation. Ever since youth, Louis Riel had regarded St. Joseph as a special, personal patron. In September 1884, when Bishop Grandin visited the settlements around Batoche, Riel suggested that St. Joseph be made the official patron of the Métis nation, just as St. John the Baptist was the patron of the French-Canadian nation. He also proposed that July 24, one month after the feast day of Jean-Baptiste, should become the celebration day of St. Joseph as protector of the Métis. Bishop Grandin consented to these proposals and furthermore agreed to allow a special inaugural celebration on September 24, 1884, since July 24 of that year was already past. Hence the three dates mentioned in the paragraph. The entire affair is an illustration of Riel's determination to constitute the Métis as a distinct nationality with their own identifying symbols.

The 19th day of the month of August, 1885

My God! Through the divine grace and influence of Jesus Christ, grant me all the holy attitudes of obedience in strict conformity to all Your wishes. Guide me, be with me through

Mary Immaculate and under the marvelous protection of Saint Joseph!

I ask You for everything You want me to ask for! I desire everything You want me to desire. I seek everything You want me to seek.

I submit entirely to Your divine discretion. If it is Your will that I die, I prefer to go to my death, with Your divine help, than to return to my family, no matter how much it would warm my heart to see my wife and children again, my beloved mother, my brothers and sisters, my in-laws and all those who are dear to me! My God, if the day that men have set for my death is the same day that You Yourself have chosen, then I freely accept it as the day of my last breath. Let that day come! And let it dawn amidst the chorus of the angels and the saints of heaven and of all the Church. I greet it together with Jesus Christ, with Mary Immaculate, with Saint Joseph and with my patron saints.

O my God! Detach me, through Jesus Christ, from everything which is not part of You.

If it is Your will that I end my life on the 18th of this September, may it be praised and blessed forever! With Your help, through the divine grace and influence of Jesus Christ, under the magnificent protection of Mary and Saint Joseph, I hasten to execute Your orders. I rejoice in the wishes of Your all-loving Providence.

In the name of the Father and the Son and the Holy Ghost!

Meditation on Judgment

How does it happen that we deceive ourselves so easily about the question of judgment? When we do evil, the great care we take to conceal it is an effort to try to escape from judgment.

Why do we hide ourselves in the first place? Because we have judged ourselves, because we have acted badly. Besides, we assume that if our neighbour were informed of the nature of our conduct, he would condemn us too. Such an assessment is clear and well-reasoned. And if we die in that state, under the weight of the judgments which we have passed upon ourselves, do we think that our soul will be acquitted before God, who never fails to notice even the least nuance of our thoughts? How can we cherish the illusion that what we ourselves condemn, which our neighbours cannot help but condemn, is perhaps going to slip by unnoticed when the Infinite Himself passes judgment on us?

Confession is the great remedy for all the remorse, all the doubts, all the despondency of the human heart.

Christians, whoever you are, go to confession, and your burden will be eased; your moral sufferings will be greatly diminished. And if you faithfully follow the guidance of your good confessor, your self-reproach will give way to peace of mind. In a little while the attentive and pious prayers of your souls, together with repentance and mortification, will reconcile you to God and . . . *(page torn out)*.

. . . what he did during his militant life.

O my God! Through the divine grace and influence of Jesus Christ, give me perfect obedience, that I may follow the priest; that I may address him according to his concerns and moods; that, according to Christian love of duty, he may be pleased to support my views and ideas; and that it may be to his great advantage to second me in all I have to do. For his part, give him the grace to address me in the most proper and fitting way in order to make me work pleasingly, joyously, energetically, without stopping, with all sorts of divine and human effectiveness, for Your greater glory, for the honour of religion, for the triumph of truth, for the salvation of all men of good will and for the improvement of the condition of all those who are opposed to us.

O Mary, queen conceived without sin, pray for me, pray for us.

O Saint Joseph, our great protector, chosen patron of the Métis, patron of the universal Church, intercede for us; protect me, protect us.

Death has gained a day on me since yesterday.

Death is now busily taking today away from me.

Death is stealing my time as fast as the pendulum of the

clock can count the seconds. My God, help me to get ready!

The priest leads me to life. Obedience to his advice is the right path.

The Christian who faithfully obeys his confessor with motives of sincere devotion will be saved, even if he to whom he confesses is not in the state of grace.

On the contrary, let your confessor be a man of high perfection, as high as you can imagine. If you do not pay close attention to what he says, you will be lost, while he will win a beautiful crown in Heaven.

Redemption is a mystery of mercy.

A priest can save many people and yet be lost himself. A priest can lose many souls; nonetheless, with true repentance at the right time, he can be entirely converted to God and re-enter into all God's favours, through the mercy of Jesus Christ.

O my God! Fill Your clergy with the most edifying virtue. Bestow on them, through Jesus Christ, the most admirable faith in Your works and in all that You wish to accomplish.

My God! I offer you the performance of the stations of the cross which I do in union with Jesus Christ, in community of feeling with Mary, Your Mother of Sorrow, for the expiation of all my sins, to sanctify myself and prepare for a good death, begging You to mercifully bless all whom I hold dear in this world and begging You to succour and deliver today, at this very second, all those in Purgatory whom I hold dear.

My God! Since it seems to me that making the stations of the cross is so pleasing in Your sight because of the very pious hommage rendered to the passion of Your Beloved Son, our Saviour, I will multiply my intentions and my prayers in the confidence that You will hear me at the foot of the crucifix through the holy intercession of Mary Immaculate. Please succour and deliver today, at this very second, the souls of the Indians, Métis, French-Canadians and Frenchmen who are in Purgatory. Deign to make all the Indians, Métis, French-Canadians and Frenchmen of the world eager right now for the exclusive colonization of Manitoba by French-Canadian Métis.

In the margin: My communion for the intention of the prayer contained on these pages.

Please succour and deliver today, at this very second, the souls of the Irish who are in Purgatory. Deign to make all the Irish of the world eager right now for the foundation of a New Ireland in the North-West.

Please succour and deliver the souls of the Italians who are in Purgatory. Deign to make all the Italians of the world eager right now for the foundation of a New Italy in the North-West.

Please succour and deliver today, at this very instant, the souls of the Bavarians who are in Purgatory. Deign to make all the Bavarians of the world eager right now for the foundation of a New Bavaria in the North-West. Please, O my God, succour and deliver today, at this very second, the souls of the Poles who are in Purgatory. Deign to make all the Poles of the world eager right now for the foundation of a New Poland in Saskatchewan — immediately, without delay.

My God, please succour and deliver, through Jesus, Mary and Joseph today, at this very second, the souls of the Belgians, Swedes, Norwegians and Danes who are in Purgatory. Deign to make the Belgians eager right now for the foundation of a New Belgium on Vancouver Island; and deign to make the three related branches of the fine Scandinavian family, the Swedes, Norwegians and Danes, eager right now for the foundation of a New Scandinavia in British Columbia.

My God! Please succour and deliver through Jesus, Mary and Joseph today, at this very instant, the souls of the Jews who are in Purgatory. Deign to make all the Jews of the world eager from now on for the foundation of a New Judea on the shores of the Pacific, in accordance with the views which You mercifully helped me to set forth before the court at Regina the first day of the month of August 1885.

Riel conveyed this theory of immigration to the Métis before and during the rebellion and consistently maintained it afterwards. It was probably developed in Riel's mind after he became acquainted with the Catholic Colonization Bureau of John Ireland, bishop of St. Paul, Minnesota.

My God! I offer You through Jesus Christ my death sentence, my captivity, my chains, the weight of my chains, my privations, my anxieties and my sufferings, as well as the confession and communion which I wish to make today. Help me to place myself under the miraculous protection of Saint Joseph, under the admirable and splendid protection of Mary. Bless my confession, accept my communion. I am united to my confessor. I am united to him during the celebration of the Mass. I desire everything that he desires in Your name. I wish to do everything which he commands me in his capacity as minister of Jesus Christ. Please give me joy according to the intentions of Your Providence which we love even when they are beyond our measure.

Do it in Your fatherly love tomorrow and the day after; give me joy, O my God; put me under the infinite protection of the merits of Jesus Christ, under the splendid protection of Mary, in the wonderful keeping of the Blessed Virgin, under the ever-effective protectorate of Saint Joseph, the chosen patron of the Métis and the patron of the universal Church.

My God! Through Jesus Christ my Saviour, grant me the favour of gaining, under the safeguard of Mary and Joseph, the plenary indulgence which the holy Catholic Church gives me the opportunity of obtaining today, since I have the signal good fortune of going to communion. Guide me, charitably help me in the recitation of the prayer which I must recite to obtain that plenary indulgence. And in Your mercy deign to apply it to the aid and the immediate deliverance of the souls of the Indians, Métis, French-Canadians, French, Irish, Italians, Bavarians, Poles, Belgians, Swedes, Norwegians, Danes and Hebrews who are in Purgatory. And, through the blessed effects of our devotion to the cause of those dear suffering souls, deign to make me succeed in the important business of my temporal and eternal salvation. You Yourself, Almighty God, through the divine influence of Your only Son, Jesus Christ, inspire all the Indians, Métis, French-Canadians, French, Irish, Italians, Bavarians, Poles, Swedes, Norwegians, Danes, Belgians and

Hebrews of the whole world with enthusiasm for Your great plans. Command them all, through the irresistible power of Jesus Christ, to eagerly support my projects: particularly inspire the Indians, Métis, French-Canadians and French with enthusiasm for the pure French-Canadian-Métis colonization of Manitoba; the Irish, Italians, Bavarians and Poles for the foundation of a New Ireland, of a New Italy, of a New Bavaria, of a New Poland in the North-West to the east of the Rocky Mountains; the Swedes, Norwegians, Danes, Belgians and Hebrews for the foundation of a New Sweden, of a New Norway, of a New Denmark, of a New Belgium and of a New Judea in the North-West to the west of the Rocky Mountains — thanks to the perpetual help of Mary Immaculate, thanks to the ineffable favour which Saint Joseph enjoys before Mary, Jesus and God Himself.

In the margin: O my God, communion has such a divine value — I offer You my communion, begging You to grant the entreaties which my soul directs to You in the prayer written here.

And in the margin of the next page: O Jesus, Mary and Joseph, present my communion to God yourselves, asking Him to grant mercifully the prayer contained on these pages.

The Conservatives of the eastern provinces are quaking with fear. The disturbance which is upsetting them is at least four times greater than that of '74.[9] The members of the party of the right are indignant, they are mutinous, they are kicking up a fuss. The leaders are starting to admit that the treaty of '70 was not observed, that they have not fulfilled their obligations.

But the Liberals have taken the lead, especially in Lower Canada. They are in full cry. They have their opponents over a barrel. The leaders of the government party, even the most important among them, are in such a pickle that they openly confess how they have broken faith with me, the Métis and the whole North-West.

If the death sentence passed against me were carried out, I

9. A reference to the Canadian Pacific Railway scandal.

think that there would be no Conservative newspaper, not even the oldest or the most avowedly "blue," which would not be overcome with pain and chagrin. I can hear them declaiming about the martyr to arbitrary power. They would be speaking of me when they said in the name of Lower Canada: "Our beloved Louis Riel has been executed!" And look what else I see!

Just consider how agitated the rest of the press must be, if the current state of opinion already allows one to surmise and predict, with a fair degree of certainty, that even the government newspapers are only a step or two from throwing aside all reserve.

It is becoming impossible for the Conservatives to maintain themselves in power.

Fortunately for them, it seems to me that a way out has been prepared for them through the work of Providence.

I am confident that, if God sustains me through the divine grace and power of Jesus Christ, the Conservatives are going to march in the path of providential ideas, to make their policies conform to sounder notions of justice and to repair a good part of the public damage which they have caused in the last fifteen years.

That, in my opinion, is the trend of politics in the eastern provinces as of today, August 21, 1885.

Glory be to the Father, to the Son and to the Holy Spirit! As it was in the beginning, is now and ever shall be, world without end. Amen.

Death hovers over me like a great bird of prey flying over a chicken which it wants to carry off.

Death keeps guard at the door of my cell.

Death peers at me behind my prison bars.

Death watches at my door like a Labrador retriever keeping watch in front of the house.

I believe that things are going badly for Sir John A. Macdonald, that the Honourable Hector Langevin is not complacent any more.

The burden of the situation lies heavily upon Edward Blake.

The two old parties have reached the end of the line.

August 22, 1885

Death destroys the trees around me. She takes her victims from among my livestock. Even if I sacrifice one of the animals from my flocks, I become an instrument of death.

The language of death is eloquent. It is a language expressed in facts, not figures of speech. The birds of the air are subject to the laws of mortality. The fish hiding in the fathomless depths of the oceans are not concealed from death.

Man, whom God has placed at the head of creation, will obey death because he has disobeyed his Creator. Death! It is sin which has invited you into the world. You did not keep us waiting; it was not long after the invitation that you made your appearance. You are our guest. You deserve a kind and warm reception, for you only come to us after being summoned. Man has made a deliberate choice between immortality and mortality; and in exercising his freedom, he has consented to be your servant. Death, you have power over him because he has chosen you to be his mistress; it is fair that you should be obeyed. I am getting ready to receive you whenever it pleases God to send you to me. For imperious as you are, Death, you are subject to a power which must be acknowledged and obeyed — the absolute power of the One who, being life itself, has nothing which belongs to you; the sovereign power of the all-loving God without whose permission you cannot approach me.

Meditation on Hell

Hell! Where is its abyss? Is it deep? Is it frightful? Yes, the pit of hell is deep and frightful. The Gospel lets us know what horrible torments must be endured there by the damned. The wicked rich man says to Lazarus that he is tortured by flames. Jesus Christ reveals to us: in that place there is weeping and gnashing of teeth, the gnawing worm devours and the fire is never extinguished.

Hell is a fire which has no end. The Gospel warns us well. Jesus Christ Himself is the one who teaches us to fear that place of suffering.

Christians! Let us reflect upon it!

My God! Through the divine grace and power of Jesus Christ, according to the blessings which I continually beseech You to pour forth on the nations, the peoples, the tribes, the families and the individuals of the earth: deign to grant me in this world, through Jesus Christ and under the protection of Mary and Saint Joseph, recompense a hundred times over for the blessings which I ceaselessly try to invoke upon my wife, my children, my mother, my father-in-law, my mother-in-law, my brothers, my sisters, my brothers-in-law, my sisters-in-law, my nephews, my nieces, my uncles, my aunts, my cousins, all my relatives, neighbours, friends and those who do good to me; upon the Vicar of Jesus Christ on earth, all bishops and ordained priests, especially all people, ecclesiastics and laymen, who have greatly loved us and who still greatly love us before You and before men; who have done us the most good and still do us the most good, in Your presence, O my God, and in the presence of my neighbour. And, O my God, please compensate me mercifully through Jesus Christ, under the protection of Mary Immaculate, through the intercession of Saint Joseph, by making the benedictions which I beg from You every day on behalf of my neighbours from one end of the world to the other redound to my benefit in eternal life.

My God! Bless my enemies greatly. I make this sincere prayer in union with Jesus Christ, with the Blessed Virgin, with Saint Joseph. If my enemies obstinately refuse the great blessings which I ask You to give them, let that same blessing, through the infallible word of Christ, descend upon the children of peace who are among them and upon me, being multiplied a hundredfold in this world and obtaining eternal life for us as soon as we breathe our last!

I trust in God that Death cannot easily overtake me and that Jesus Christ will not let her put her hand on me, because of my charity toward the Reverend Father J.-V. Fourmond who humiliated me as much as he could. May the Good Lord spread His most merciful benediction upon him in return.[10]

Because of the good which I wish for him and am asking for him, through the merits of Jesus Christ, through the intercession of Mary and Joseph, I am confident that God is going to help me escape soon from the bitterness of my suffering; that His mercy is going to aid me; and that I will easily leap, safe and sound, over the abyss of difficulties which is my present situation; that I will quickly surmount all obstacles; and that before long I will reach safety. I am sacrificing my own will in order to demonstrate unmistakably my love and my profoundly religious respect towards approved priests and bishops. I am paid back in a way as consoling as it is wonderful! The divine influence of Jesus Christ, the protection of Mary and that of Saint Joseph dispose French Canada to stand beside me in my troubles, to be with me in my dangers. They send me great help from various nationalities. The power of Jesus Christ, the divine power of God's Son, the consolations of Mary Immaculate, the marvelous care of Saint Joseph enable me to walk dryshod across the river of sorrow, and help me to glide over the roughest spots on my road, as if I were on a streetcar.

Has not the Crown made copies of the most important of my documents? I think so.

August 23, 1885

For some days the Tories have been worrying about the question of my rights; but they are so touchy on that subject that they did not dare to face it squarely. They were frustrated. They went this way and that. Yesterday, I think they finally got down to openly discussing the blow which I struck for my

10. Riel has in mind the recantation drawn up by Fourmond.

rights in Saskatchewan. They spoke at length about it. There is decency in the Tories.

Most of them are starting to come out in my favour.

I have the strong impression that a considerable movement is stirring in the ranks of the Conservative party with a view to promoting the interests of my mission. Many of them, thank God, have faith in the validity of my task. They do not conceal their belief that I am sent by God. And if I am not mistaken, the episcopacy and the clergy, who are resolved not to do anything against Rome, would be happy if the tide of current events carried them along, and by a marvelous series of uncontrollable eventualities, becoming ever more inescapable, miraculously gave them the reasons and arguments they need to maintain that my mission and theirs are one and the same; that my mission is an outgrowth of theirs; that consequently my mission, coming from Jesus Christ through their ministry, can in justice not be considered apart from their mission.

If I understand the situation properly, the political and religious wind which is blowing throughout the North is going to furnish the Catholic Church the two wings needed to take flight amidst the sublime destinies of the New World. And with the help of God, through Jesus Christ His beloved Son and our divine Saviour, the holy Catholic Church, my mother, will not be able to delay in embracing me openly and proclaiming with joy and gentleness that I am the fruit of her womb. And profoundly contrite for having severely tested me these fifteen long years, she will bless God for having sustained me. Her heart's voice, maternal and always inspired, will make me ascend to the impregnable citadel of her benedictions. The spouse of Christ, the Church, my mother, will shower me with her own blessings. Her solicitude will honour me because I, little David in the service of the great King, had the courage to go outside the camp of Israel for a moment, to try to hold off the giant who was marching against all of us with his redoubtable strength and reputation.

I think that the ten nationalities which I have recognized in my thinking are happy. I understand that they are at work.

They are aroused on both sides of the border.[11]

It is funny how the Liberals are pleased with me in the [United] States. And through the divine power of Jesus Christ, the Conservatives are not afraid of me. And they see that my views are essentially compatible with their own best interests.

For the time being, the Liberals are happier on my account than the Conservatives, at least I believe so.

Recently people have been heaping many reproaches on my back. How the accusations weighed on me! But yesterday, it did not take long, the knowledge of a well-intentioned man exonerated me and cleared me almost totally.

I have helped the clergy; the clergy help me. I have exculpated them; they exculpate me in turn. Their charitable hand is busy wiping from my face the many insults hurled at me.

The following paragraph has been crossed out, perhaps because Riel or his confessor, Father André, found it too presumptuous: The clergy deplore . . .[?] all those of my actions which they do not understand. But before long the living warmth of Catholicism is going to dry their tears and make them evaporate, I hope, from this day forth. I am confident of it.

The opposition members used strong words yesterday. If the government does not pay attention, their opponents could resort to language even more threatening than yesterday.

The clergy spoke aloud from the pulpit today. They had the charity to intervene on my behalf. They are urging the faithful to demand a pardon, to request royal clemency for me.

Blessed be the angels of mercy!

My God! Through the divine compassion of Jesus Christ, remit all my sins and all the punishment due to my sins; all my faults and all the consequences of my faults; all my offences and all the results of my offences.

In the margin: Communion on August 26 for the intention of the prayer written here.

O Death! I see crowds striving to defend me from your

11. Riel refers to the Irish, Poles, Bavarians, etc., whom he wished to bring to the North-West.

hand. People are swarming to keep you from taking me now. In the name of Christ who overcame you, be gone from me. I still have work to do for the greatest glory of my God, for the most brilliant honour of religion, for the shining triumph of truth, for my own exemplary happiness in this world and the next, for the redemption of men of good will, for the improvement of the condition of my enemies.

O good Death! O my friend! While you wait for me, be kind enough to stay far away (or at least what seems far to our human eyes). Wait for me, O my friend. O edifying Death, accompanied by all the succours of the Church, wait for me on the path of the most beautiful and happiest old age. Through the infinite merits of Jesus Christ, under the protection of Mary, under the protection of Saint Joseph, through those three kind persons who pleased you and loved you, I promise you the crown of my white hair, God willing. If my Creator, Almighty God, and my Saviour, the Christ of life, deign to prolong my days and years until that time, O Christian and all-consoling Death whom I claim as my own, I will meet you when my beard is white as snow and its brilliant whiteness gladdens the sight of those who see you. I will go to find the repose and sleep of resurrection in your strong arms, when my eyebrows are the same colour as the flowers on the priest's alb and my eyelashes have become as pure as the fringe of a white flag.

Happy is he who carefully compares the intensity of his physical pains, of his moral sufferings, with what the Gospel reveals to us about the pains of hell: the fear of God will fill his conscience and make him better!

Happy is he who seeks knowledge of divine pleasures: to the extent that he discovers their charms, he becomes more desirous of them. Putting his foot firmly on each step, he easily ascends the entire ladder of happiness!

My God! Through the divine grace of Jesus Christ, guide and mercifully show my wife how to raise our little children, the precious little children You have given us. Let her make them behave at meals; let her make them understand at an early age the advantages of temperance in eating and drinking. O Mary, who raised Jesus Christ, have the charity to teach my wife how you set about molding the heart of Your Son (to the extent that He was man).

Saint Joseph, bless my wife that she may be a Christian mother most pleasing to God in everything, always and everywhere, but particularly in seeing to the education of her children.

In the margin: Communion on the 26th of the month of August for the intention of the prayer written here.

My God! I have given Jesus Christ His place, I am sure. O my God! Through Jesus Christ, deign to give me my place, the place that You gave me and men have taken away.

I have the distinct impression that the biggest businessmen of the Liberal party, even those who usually hold themselves aloof from politics, are coming into the movement of the North. They are agreeing to occupy high places in the various organizations. It is truly something out of the ordinary.

My God! I offer You through Jesus Christ my death sentence, my imprisonment, my chains, the weight of my chains, my privations, my pains, my sufferings. I join them to the passion of our beloved Saviour that it may please You, because of His infinite merits, to pour out Your divine Spirit on all men and to renew the face of the earth.

Save me with the help of the prayers of Mary and Saint Joseph.

Dictate to me Yourself, O my God, the petition which I am writing now, through Jesus Christ. May the graces of Mary's prayers penetrate my spirit and help me to write it well. May the favourable intercession of Saint Joseph as well as the requests of Saint Louis and the holy King David obtain from Your mercy the favour of formulating it exactly as You wish, not only that it may lead to the salvation of men and to their greatest edification, but also that it may be a salutary document with respect to my most precious interests in time and eternity, a document rich in utility for the most splendid glory of God, for the purest honour of religion and the triumph of truth.

In the margin: 26th of the month of August. I offer You, O my God, my confession and today's communion for the intention of the prayer written here, and in general that You may deign to hear all the prayers with which my soul is filled.

The petition to which Riel refers is probably the document which he sent to President Grover Cleveland of the United States, requesting him to annex the North-West Territories.

August 25, 1885

My God! I thank You for having accorded me the favour of celebrating this day in honour of Saint Louis, my glorious patron. Please hear the vows and prayers I address to You through the mediation of Your servant whom the Church has canonized. It is a signal honour to bear his name. I sincerely believe he is the most glorious of the kings who have governed France. The activities of his life were so virtuous that You were pleased to place him high in the esteem of men and nations. Saint Louis! Pray for me. And all you saints of heaven who bore the name of Louis during your life here below, I am glad to stand behind the shield of your charitable intercession. But above all, you who gave me life, O Louis my father, whom I believe to be in Paradise, who surrendered your soul to God amidst all the help provided by the Church, amidst prayers and in the sanctuary of sentiments most congenial to Jesus Christ, cast your affectionate paternal glance upon me. Bless me with a benediction most ample, precious, great and abundant. Please make the blessings of Jesus, Mary and Saint Joseph, as well as your own, descend upon me and my wife and children — blessings which can banish the evils with which I am threatened and which hang over my family as well as my fellow countrymen. Saint Louis, protect me continuously. Do not abandon me either day or night. Obtain for me from God the ineffable grace of accomplishing in all respects what is most pleasing, and of receiving even in this world compensation for the efforts and labour which I have expended for His greater glory, for the honour of religion, for the triumph of truth, for my greater happiness in this life as well as in the future life, for the edification of my neighbour from one end of the world to the other, and for the amelioration of the condition of those who forget You, O my God. Saint Louis, my beloved patron, the most beloved among the elect of God, tenderly embrace me with your heavenly affection, that the enemy may never prevail against me.

In the space between the preceding paragraph and the following, Riel has inserted these sentences: Jesus, Mary, Joseph, save Magnus Burston. To Jesus, Mary and Joseph I offer my prayers for Magnus Burston.[12]

I think there will be a manoeuvre to prove that my actions are deprived of moral liberty. But maybe God will not let that expedient succeed.

Some other human event is waiting for me and can take place to save my life, to save my health, liberty and reputation.

O my God! Please protect my friend Gabriel Dumont. Through Jesus, Mary and Joseph, lead him in the right path of temporal and eternal salvation. Do not let him fall into confusion, but have the mercy to keep him in great honour because of the blessing which Your priest gave him in accordance with the intentions of Your Providence, which we love even when they surpass our understanding.[13]

My God! You know which good qualities are in every man, bless those good qualities in each person. Bless my guards, my adversaries, even those who do not regard me with favour. Bless them all.

26th of the month of August 1885

Why is not the feast of the Sacred Heart of Mary more revered? I think it is neglected.

O Mary conceived without sin! Re-kindle the fire of devotion in Christians towards your mother's heart.

My God! I give You thanks, through Jesus Christ, under the protection of Mary and Saint Joseph, for the favours You have bestowed on my son Jean, for lavishing upon him from

12. Burston was then awaiting trial for his alleged participation in the rebellion.
13. Riel refers to a blessing given by Father Eberschweiler, S.J., in Montana in June 1884.

earliest infancy a strong sense of Your justice. Lord, foster in him the natural and supernatural love of justice which You have mercifully given him — a love of its thoughts and intentions, of upright speech, of the free play of the interests of justice.

August 27, 1885

My God! My proposal, my intention, my resolution is fixed: I address to the name of Jesus, Mary and Joseph all my prayers, orisons, ejaculations; all my thoughts, words, desires, writings and actions today, together with my sufferings of any kind. Please find them worthy. My aim in addressing all this to You in the name of Jesus, Mary, Joseph and my patron saints, is that You may be pleased to display Your greatest glory, the most beautiful honour of religion, the most consoling triumph of truth; that You may be pleased to secure my prompt and immediate liberation, my most flourishing prosperity, my greater happiness in this world and next, my temporal and eternal salvation, the redemption of men of good will and the improvement of the condition of all others.

Accept my intentions today, and please find them worthy tomorrow, the day after and all the days of my life. Thus I consecrate them to You, my God, at the present moment. I beg You through Jesus, Mary and Joseph to set me at liberty. My God! Keep me Yourself in unchanging calm, through Jesus, Mary and Joseph. Keep me ready for whatever happens, ready to succeed and triumph as well as to die, ready to die as well as to conquer and triumph in You and through You.

My God! Grant me, through the divine grace, mercy and light of Jesus Christ, the favour of seeing my inner self realistically and of recognizing myself in Your presence. Lavish upon me all the riches of Your grace, all the gifts and fruits of Your Spirit. Make me sure of the good which is in me. Show me Yourself that what is good in me is really good. Show me my illusions; let me recognize them for illusions and let me treat them as such. If there are worthy things in me which men have made me doubt, please let me see them in their true light. Help me preserve and perfect them.

My God, give me Your reason, the sound reason of a good conscience, so that I regulate my meals properly, so that I fittingly adjust the quantity of my eating and drinking to the necessity of keeping up my strength and being ready to do whatever You wish.

Jesus, my beloved Saviour, bless me, I ask in Your name, bless me with my wife and my children, with my relatives and friends. Place Your most holy benediction on our food, our clothing, our homes and all our pleasures, that we may always be temperate and modest, with sincerity and without affectation, and that we may gain the happiness of Paradise in heaven through a simple Christian life, wisely apportioned between ease and austerity. O Mary, Mother of Mercy so influential with God, come to my help. Offer my prayers to God that He may have the paternal charity to hear them. Saint Joseph! O my great protector, chosen patron of the Métis, patron of the universal Church, intercede for us by presenting to the Lord our humble requests and our earnest supplications.

My God! I give You thanks for the advice with which you inspire me through Jesus Christ. Be with me that I may draw great benefit from it. Oh! Help me to write a good and just petition. Help me to scrutinize it with careful attention. Help me to avoid dubious arguments. Help me through Jesus Christ, help me under the protection of Mary and Saint Joseph, under the benedictions of my blessed patrons. May I be united heart and soul to my Archbishop and my confessor. Lead me Yourself, assist me Yourself in the choice of my arguments. Help me to make them stand out and to guide them with a sure hand as one hurls a spear at a target. Send Your angels to my aid at the right time.

August 28, 1885

Circumstances make it advisable to do what I would prefer not to.

My God! Support me with Your wisdom. Your Providence has foreseen all, prepared all. Blessed be Your Providence in all things, always and everywhere!

Bless me in my choice! As Your Spirit told me: "Be blessed in your choice!" Let my choice be Yours. O my God! O my Saviour, Jesus!

My God! Bless me according to Your infinite goodness!

Inspire me Yourself, through Jesus, Mary and Joseph! Inspire all my leadership, all my politics, all my diplomacy!

Through Jesus, Mary and Joseph, lend Your inspiration to all my talent, to all the wisdom of my talent. Give me a most extraordinary talent for peace. Lavish upon me the most marvelous wisdom of a talent for peace. Through Jesus, Mary and Joseph, protect me Yourself, with my wife, with my innocent little children, with all whom I hold dear in this world. Safeguard me Yourself with my spouse and my children; with my kind mother, so affectionate and beloved; with all my brothers and sisters, with all brothers- and sisters-in-law; with all whom I hold dear on earth; with my lawyers; with all of New France; with my whole nation; with the whole Church.

My God! Enlighten me Yourself, sustain me Yourself, through the merciful wisdom and power of Jesus Christ; and make me compose the declaration or petition that You want from me. Help me Yourself to formulate it according to Your Holy Spirit of truth, integrity, justice, accuracy, expeditious speed, true appropriateness, precision, conciseness, lucidity, clarity, logic, eloquence, poetry, wide experience, irresistible authority.

In Latin: Jesus, sun of justice, save me! Mary, mirror of justice, pray for us. Saint Joseph, intercede for us who venerate you . . . *(end of text).*

7 Imprisonment
October 1885

Riel's August diary exhibited his determination to subordinate himself entirely to the will of the church as communicated to him by his spiritual advisors, first Fathers Fourmond and Cochin, then Father André. However, by October that resolution had weakened considerably. Riel had recommenced his prophetic activities and was receiving fresh revelations almost daily. Father André, despairing of being able to suppress totally this prophetic exuberance, was content to use his authority to keep Riel within the bounds of orthodoxy. He made Riel retract any revelations which conflicted with Catholic doctrine, but did not interfere with prophecies which were not heretical. Riel, for his part, seems to have been satisfied with this compromise. As will be seen in the last part of this chapter, he made a serious effort to revise his thinking in order to render it compatible with Catholic teaching.

Except for the last section, it is difficult to typify the October diary. Riel used it to enter his thoughts (or "revelations") almost in random fashion. It contains relatively few of the longer, carefully written compositions which are so predominant in the August manuscript. For unexplained reasons, there are numerous departures from strict chronological order, which I have not tried to alter in this edition of the text. It may well be that sometimes Riel jotted down his revelations on loose scraps of paper at the time of inspiration, and then later copied them into the bound notebook, dating them according to the day when they were first written down. Such a procedure might account for the disjointed chronology in the notebook.

Although it is admittedly difficult to generalize, on the whole this month's diary has a much more optimistic tone than its August counterpart. Riel seems to have felt that so much popular support for his

143

cause was developing that the cabinet would be forced to commute his sentence. No longer expecting to die, he looked forward to resuming his "mission" as "prophet of the New World," communicating his revelations to the people of the Americas.

October 2, 1885

God made me see that I was climbing the holy mountain step by step. Mankind was to help me ascend it. The things men were doing on my behalf put me in a joyful and encouraging state of mind. Although I was walking carefully, I was serene, not anxious. Gigantic forces were going ahead of me. Without appearing to do so, I was guiding them. They were clearing my path without intending to. These powers were continually treading on some infernal plot or other. They passed by hearths of diabolical conspiracy, which fortunately lost their fires almost as soon as I noticed them. My path was the same as the path of the friendly powers; and that path was narrow, hardly wide enough for my two feet. Almighty God had things in His keeping. "I am coming to the end of my trials. Blessed be the French-Canadian. Blessed be the French-speaking Italian in the United States. It is they who make me escape from my difficulties and distress."

Although Riel put these last sentences in quotation marks, it is not apparent what they are quoted from.

Louis "David" Riel

It is the hand of God which has led me up the path around the holy mountain, climbing step by step! Now that I have my bearings, the virtuous Italian and the French-Canadian are helping me travel through the valleys and lowlands of humanity.

It is the Church which speaks through me.

The humble and virtuous Italian is admirably kind and simple. He can lead me to a glorious peace. The French-Canadian is a man of God.

This rather obscure allegory is not actually contained in Riel's diary, but was found on a separate sheet of paper. Its interpretation is far from clear. Riel's path around the mountain obviously represents his divine mission, but who are "the French-Canadian" and "the French-speaking Italian in the United States?" Perhaps these figures do not stand for individuals but are allegorical types designating respectively the French-Canadian Catholic Church and the Francophone Church of the Canadian diaspora in the United States. In that case, the word "Italian" would signify the church's continued loyalty to Rome.

October 3, Morning
Prophecies

Who is the tall dark woman? Who is the strong pregnant woman who tells me: "After twenty-two days, it will all be over?"

She is a woman with a long face, a square forehead and chin, and a beautiful, striking figure. Who is she? She is a Métisse. But who? O pregnant women, pray to the Blessed Virgin, that she may visit you with her protection as she visited Saint Elizabeth. The birth of your child is a danger to you; if God does not protect you, who will save you?

O my God! If You wish, You can save us and prolong our days and help us to raise our dear little children in the sanctity of Your service. Through Jesus, Mary and Joseph, please make us live. O my God! Save my dear wife. Instruct her.

At this time, Riel's wife Marguerite was expecting a baby in late October. The child, born on the twenty-first of the month, lived only a few hours.

Revelations of October 6, 1:00 P.M.

Between the Frenchman and me and the *Canadien* we know something.

The man in guard's uniform, the one who was neglecting me, suddenly is startled. He shrinks back with a long face.

Quickly he comes near me. He turns smartly towards me. One can tell by his expression how anxious he is. He tries to understand.

Blessed be guards who do their Christian duty!

Hear the word of the Lord: the late___[?] was to(*sic*) small for me; did not shine for me; was opposed to me; trode (*sic*) under foot my table, the Holy Eucharist; was again the Blessed Virgin. It was the little___[?] of the left. I have left it.

This whole paragraph was written in English. Riel later blotted out two key words, making it impossible to identify the person he was writing about.

In their marvelous dance, I see Indians coming from the East and reaching the West, under the impulse of Conservative influences.

The true Church is composed of those who sacrifice themselves to rescue men of good will, as at the time of the Apostles.

It is the Church who places herself squarely between her children and aggressors.

It is the Church who has zeal and who ceaselessly defends the true interests of the flock.

The divine Essence reveals to me that the North-West is passing to the United States. And I say: "When the United States neglect you, the Métis children of Manitoba, led by the finger of God, will go to be educated in the Spanish countries of the New World. During their studies, the voice of God will speak to them. They will help the Spanish lands recover their strength. Bards will lift their voices, and the Spanish peoples will be aroused by the sacred songs. They will fly to the rescue of the North-West and of New France.

Revelations on Brief Subjects

Emperors and princes will accept my ideas. They will apply them to fulfill my intentions, to do my work.

Two paragraphs have been crossed out and are illegible except for the closing words: humble little Louis "David" Riel.

He could give his life; he has not given it.

Parable

A father of a family had a son six or seven years old, small for his age and weak. But he could speak.

That child was destined to death and to the torment of fire.

His father came to him. Seeing the boy, he felt love for his son. But remembering that he had fathered the child by a woman who was not his true wife, he thought it would be better not to caress him. Since he intended to kill the boy and throw him into the fire, treating him tenderly would make it too painful to carry out his cruel plan. However, he said to him, "Well, try." The child responded with indifference, "I know that you are everything." He added a few more words which indirectly implied, "I hardly care about it," or "It doesn't bother me much." It would have been too heartless to say such things openly. But the child was naturally so unfeeling that he made his meaning clear. Nevertheless, he turned as his father wished and knelt as best he could.

What kind of father is that? What kind of child?

What sort of father prostituted himself with a woman who was not his legitimate wife? What sort of mother would have given birth to an illegitimate son? Who is that illegitimate child? Oh! Reflect, see the deep meaning of this parable. O you ministers of the various faiths! O you who belong to any faith! O you numerous Christian denominations, I pray you in the name of the Son of God, our Saviour, study what I wish to tell you, for it is necessary for you to understand it well.

The Spirit of God made me say: "I am not saying I will live to old age, but I think so. I still have time. I know that many people will enthusiastically support my projects."

The spirit of God said to me: "These men are corrupt and spendthrift."

Revelations of October 14 - 15, 1885

The Power of God leads me in the spirit of righteousness. Complete and perfect confession transports me to a great height, where I can see far and wide.

147

I am the banner of the Lord. He bears me like a flag unfurled.

All the *bleus* having retired from public affairs, all the *bleus* having withdrawn into private life, I go from door to door among the greatest houses, teaching the ways of virtue, teaching the essence of Christianity.

People accept me everywhere. My wife and my children are well-received. People believe in my mission. They admire the marvelous revelations of the Holy of Holies about things unknown since the fall of our first parents, since the beginning of the world.

As I was leaving St. Peter's mission, the Spirit of God made me say: "If I knew English, I would stay, even if the United States only published ten percent of my writings." And I added: "I will remember the Helena *Herald.* I will remember the *Herald.*"

There is a great insurrection in the North-West; the American administration was bad.

I hear the voice of the priest of St. Antoine de Padua,[14] who says to the rebels in prison: "That is going to be hard to arrange. Some men will be sentenced to thirteen, fourteen years of prison; they will be scattered, sent to different prisons in the United States." I saw a prisoner who said nothing. He was condemned to death. But the government was in more danger than he was.

Revelation

There is a way; but not now (*in English*).

I saw Eastwood Jackson. He came to see me. I was in prison and yet I was free, in my own home. I must have been out on bail. I said, "Come see me." "No," he replied, "from now on I will not visit you as much as I used to." He wanted to spend the night but he refrained from saying so. He contented himself with letting me see it. The bed that I had made for him in

14. Father Moulin.

politics was rather hard. However, I wish him well. I tell him: "Let me get out of my difficulties, let me exonerate myself, and you will see what I will do for you."

On February 24, 1885, the Spirit of God revealed something consoling to me. He said: "In three or four years, you will have your lands."

The Spirit of God made me see that I had on my head the fine hat of my grand political ideas. Who is publishing my ideas on November 3, 1885? The people of the English name are pondering my political views. The grandeur of my projects astonishes and displeases them less than one might think.

O my God! I give glory to Jesus Christ Your Son and to You. I have experienced the accuracy of the good advice that Your Messiah left to each of us when He said: "Watch and pray lest temptation enter in."

I was not enough on guard; I had not prayed enough. Temptation struck me like lightning; it passed before my eyes like a cloud. It took me by storm. At the beginning of the movement I did things I should not have done. I am sorry for it. I ask pardon from God, from my Saviour. O Sovereign Master, my Father, You alone, through Jesus Christ, can correct the mistake I have made, prevent its evil results, save me from my sin and its consequences. O Mary conceived without sin! O Saint Joseph, our dear adopted father! O my Father in heaven, aid me with Your heavenly help that I may watch continually over my senses and over the course of my thoughts. Through prayer may I be fortunate enough not to yield to temptation, but to be delivered from evil through the divine mercy and power of Jesus Christ our Lord.

October 19, 1885

The Spirit of God spoke to me, and He inspired me to say with Him: (*in English*) "I will leave here next month."

Voices of the Future

I saw my brother Charles; he is happy. He is well-dressed. He is at college. He is sitting in one of the first seats in his class. He is a smart boy, but he is still young, at most twelve years old. O my brother, it is a long time since I have seen you! It is eleven years since I last embraced you. You were so little when I went away. But blessed be God who reunites us. I have taken flight on the wings of prayer. I am high in the sky. I come to you from far away. I arrive from the South and the countries of South America. You are all alone here in the North, O my brother! Nevertheless, it is good that the Spanish of the New World come to do their studies at Montreal and St. Boniface, and in return the Métis and the *Canadiens* go to study in the colleges of New Spain. Let us get acquainted in childhood. Later, when today's young people come of age, the two continents will follow each other's doings with interest. South America will hold the North in friendly admiration. And when Providence gives the glorious Spanish their turn to occupy the public stage, their beloved brothers in North America will make their cheers and prayers rise to heaven. They will jump with joy, blessing the religious zeal and gallantry of the Spanish nations.

My brother Charles is in Paradise.

My brother Charles is a man of the new faith.

My brother Charles is a man who will play a great role.

My brother Charles will exert much influence on the United Spanish States.

My brother Charles will make himself respected in the United States of Washington.

Name of Charles! How many times will you give lustre to both North and South America?

My brother Charles is a scholar. His powerful mind investigates scientific questions and resolves them to the great astonishment of Catholicism.

My brother Charles is a famous doctor of Theology.

O my God! Through Jesus Christ, the Blessed Virgin and Saint Joseph, give me light a long time; give me light longer; give me light a very long time; give me light forever.

150

Prophecies

"He will not let it happen."

O my God! Through Jesus Christ, ensure that He lets those things happen to me which are beneficial, and that He lets them come to a successful conclusion.

O my God! Through Jesus Christ, ensure that He lets nothing happen which is contrary to Your plans; and that He impedes everything which is not in conformity with Your will.

Prophecy (*in English*)

Who is the constable who comes to my cell at night, presenting me with a pair of old mitts, but warm? The constable wears a red coat and the suit of a Mounted Policeman.

Prophecies

I am picking fruit in abundance. The fruits which the Church of Saskatchewan had stored up are for me. I take them. They are ripe. They are pretty with their green leaves still clinging to the bunch. This is not questionable fruit, but certain. Yes, this fruit is reliable. Oh, how happy I am! How calm! The foundations of my building are vast and great, they are beautiful. The first floor of this enormous house, which I myself worked to construct, is a spacious floor whose rooms are well-proportioned. They are well-lighted. There are huge tables there, loaded with bread and cakes. I am given what I wish. But it is mortification which has earned all these good things for me from God. The priest is the administrator of my wealth. He is personable, he is kind, he is sincere. He does not joke. I only see bread and milk. I eat at three o'clock in the afternoon. I am strong. I am better than the big eaters!

Prophecies

My brother Charles is a famous jurist. His books are

recognized everywhere. He dies of old age. His hair is white, but of a whiteness kind and pure.

My brother Charles is a humble and inspired preacher. He converts society through the power of his sermons.

My brother Charles is a general whose victorious sword has promoted God's glory in the United States of Washington and in the United States of Columbia.

Prophecies *(in English)*

I have seen the first-minister. He adressed [*sic*] me saying: "Mr. Riel," and pronouncing my name as if written "Reel." And he said: "Is your name Reel or Riel?" I told him that it was Riel. "But you may pronounce it in English as the languish [*sic; a pun?*] wants you to do."

And when I pronounced my name, as it is pronounced in French, it struck the attention of those who were present, that it was a brillant [*sic*] name. I did, even I self, realize that it was a glorious name to tell. My name rang somewhat as a silver bell.

The first-minister was affable and gentle to me. He said, "What you want is a lawyer that will take interest in your case. Whatever may be the issue of the appeal, that is what you need. I will throw you over in Montana." (The manner in which the first-minister expressed himself here is: "I will overthrow you Montana.") And continuing to speak he added: "You may find there a good lawyer. I will give you Pounds." And when he said "pounds," I saw that he was used to carry the weight of his words with money.

The first-minister was in the wrong. I was not.

The door is wide open towards the south.

A line is blotted out here.

I saw my lawyers. They had lost. I told them my revealed interview with the first-minister. They appeared to be unable to answer. But in order not to discourage my lawyers, I told them the words that, I knew, suited them.

After this paragraph, Riel returns to the use of French.

"It appears that he is a tyrant, that 'saviour.' "

"Give me light longer."

O my God, I beg You, give me light a long time. Give me light much longer. Give me light a very long time. Give me light forever, through Jesus, Mary and Joseph!

I am supposed to say my rosary, but the compelling voice of the divine essences commands me to leave my prayers for the moment and to write.

[Meditation on Temperance]

Oh! How necessary it is to watch our appetite!

Oh! How hard it is to curb our appetite and bring it under the control of reason. Through the great difficulty I experience in mastering myself in this respect, I see how it must be hard for the rich, for those who live in abundance, to moderate their intemperance in eating and drinking.

Above all, I see that there are no speeches or sermons which can sway them. The most compelling eloquence would not have more than an hour or two of influence over their minds.

It takes a series of divine graces strong enough to re-establish freedom, to move the will in the right direction, to encourage and control the intelligence and to gladden the memory by recalling the precious joy which is obtained by moderation in eating and drinking.

Here is what the divine essences told me about this, saying: Now that you see how pitiable is the man who groans under the weight of his defects and vices; now that you know by experience how the human will, without being aided by the help of grace, is powerless to practice temperance and to do good in general, I desire and I wish you to promise Me that:

1. in praying for yourself on any subject whatsoever, you will remind yourself to pray also for all those who have to overcome the same hardships in the world as you.
2. you will be kind to sinners. You will have compassion particularly for those dear children of the Church who sin through weakness.

3. you will bear in mind that the hardest hearts have a claim on your sympathy. And in order to arouse your pity for them, picture to yourself their torments and what their suffering will be if they fall into the devouring fires of the next life!

Revelations of October 9 - 10, 1885

Who knows in how many generations?

The Spirit of God put me in touch with Philippe Garnot. He was free. He arrived from Montana where he had gone to buy a herd of longhorns. He was on this side of the South Branch [of the Saskatchewan River].

He said, "I agree with you in many respects."

"You are going to have two juries, one in England, one here. There are some who will take notice, favourable notice, of all the points which are emphasized. That's French, that is." Then he said, "You could even make some observations and revisions by putting your initials L.R. next to the points which are underlined. If you can logically write your whole name L.D.R., then it's not yet finished."

Garnot's employer was interested in me. And Philippe told me, pointing with his foot to the place where he had halted, "You are going to spend two days on this spot."

And he with whom I was at law was receptive to my overtures. I understood that if I could offer him a means of making money, he would do anything for me.

Trudel said to me, "Are you allowing me to go to the Jesuits?" I asked if that meant "to go thank God." He replied, "Ah! Certainly."

Prophecies in short sentences, detached from one another, yet connected by a single train of thought:

Their lands for trifles.

You can take flight.

Through excessive prayer.

Your portrait: I really think that one could write to you, eh?

A minister of the American government tells me in the name of the Cabinet: "You better stay here untill" (*sic; this last sentence is in English*).

God consoles me. I know I am in my own house, because my little boy comes right to his papa, he stands up, my little boy! My child, my child, your conscience is pure! Your shirt is white. Blessed be my son! Come, come, my boy. Don't talk! Be happy! He is glad! He is surprised! Today is a great day for my son. My boy, you have thrived while I was in prison. God be praised that my son Jean is in good health!

A multitude of tender feelings springs from my heart and races ahead to Jean my son, just as rays of light run ahead of the dawn to herald the full light of day.

Who will dare to make fun of the paternal caresses which the Holy Spirit inspires in me?

Woe to you who do not understand the language of perfect love because you have no heart. Watch out! For some fine morning you could get up under the crushing weight of a curse. Who would lift it from your shoulders? Restless night will end in the terrible awakening of your sins. You laughed condescendingly at my paternal affections! Your folly will make others laugh. God will hand you over to the evil spirits of insane laughter. Go! The Lord will heap on you all the evils you have made suffer as well as all those that you still wish to make me endure! There is a black cloud hanging over my head.

O you whose hearts are open to noble sentiments! Turn your attention to those little spiritual flaws which might escape you. Do not cling to them, but reproach yourself for them. Criticize your thoughtless actions. Be worthy of God's pardon.

Revelations of October 11 - 12

André Neault looks upon me favourably. He considers my case and judges me in a spirit of fairness. But yet his position toward me is such that I find myself faced with something unpleasant in his feelings.

The Dominion is like a prancing mare. She is difficult to approach. She quivers. But as I draw near, she remains calm. It is difficult to put my hand on her back. But I will stroke her, scolding her if I must. And she will let me touch her.

The Dominion is like a pretty, half-broken mare. She is hard to ride, but I will mount into the saddle and she will obey me.

That is what the Lord tells me.

I saw a wild animal go by who looked like a moose. First, it advanced from the northeast, heading towards the southwest. It had a sort of shiny colour which did not throw light on anything. Suddenly I noticed that its pace had slackened. Soon it was hardly moving. A second later, it was completely stationary. Examining it, I realized that it had no head, that it had lost its neck, that it had missed its aim, that it had been beheaded, that both forefeet had been removed. Its tail was on its back, a tail tufted with large black hair. Stupefaction and fear kept it from moving. Those who usually went along with it were in revolt against it. Oh, the Devil! The rosary had destroyed its prosperity. I saw its hindfeet, but everything was still. While I watched, it disappeared. All that remained of the monster was a memory. The Spirit of God said to me: "The Devil is in the rosary."

To be interpreted, those words must be compared to another sentence which is similar, as for example, "The Devil is in pieces."

The rosary had torn the Devil apart. The rosary had broken the Devil into as many pieces as there are beads on the rosary. The rosary with its holy chain of *ave marias* had enchained the Devil. That is what is meant by "The Devil is in the rosary."

The Spirit of God whose word is infinitely expressive . . . (*sentence breaks off*).

Revelations of the 12th and 13th

It appears that, being overwhelmed by a substantial majority, they are speaking to you now.

October 28
Prophecies

I am glad I came because you will remain here. See the great amount of property which I have earned for you through my courage, my zeal and my trust in God. You will be comfortable for a long time. O nations whom I have cherished and whom I love, I came to help you. I am going. Many young people return with me.

The Spirit of God makes me sing ideas such as these in a raised tone of voice, magnificent with ineffable sweetness:

"Marguerite still has her land."

"And all that dies, dies."

"The Métis nation which you wished to uproot still remains on the soil bestowed by Providence."

"And everything that would have damaged and impeded the intentions of God fails and disappears."

Do you want to know if you are dealing with a violent, unreasonable man? Find out first if he is a man addicted to high living. If you find that he is, you can keep that in mind in all your dealings with him. For I tell you that he is a brute to the same degree that he is a glutton.

Impurity is no less deadly; but because it is generally accompanied by remorse, at least among Catholics, it carries with it a sort of antidote, whereas gluttony stifles remorse when it takes possession of the soul. It is gluttony that makes atheists, believe me; it is gluttony which makes Voltaireans, the impious, unbelievers, hardened sinners.

It is gluttony, alas, which makes bad priests, which produces bad bishops, which makes unfaithful pontiffs.

Nothing is so materialistic as excessive eating.

It is necessary to deal gently with gluttons. Lead them to mortify themselves a little, then more. Get them to fast once, twice. When you succeed in making them fast three days in a row — Friday in honour of the passion of Christ; Saturday in honour of His burial and His divine rest; Sunday in honour of His resurrection — you can believe then that the worst is past.

Preachers, confessors, always keep in mind what I have just told you. As often as you can, you yourselves should fast on

Friday, Saturday and Sunday. And you will see that your apostolic labours will be blessed. You will convert people to God. And you will acquire a crown of glory and of life. Fasting and prayer are the two great keys to success in time and eternity. Fasting will make the banker succeed in his good investments, and will help the hermit in his pious designs for the conversion of souls. In fasting and prayer, the public man and the politician will find the unexpected resolution of their problems and difficulties.

Nothing can resist fasting when it is done with humility, sincerity and devotion.

Fasting opens prisons and releases the most hardened criminals. Fasting demolishes scaffolds. Fasting blocks insurrections and prevents rebellions.

Three or four days of fasting accomplish more than an army on the field of battle. Yes, four days of fasting, properly performed and offered to God in union with the fasting of Jesus Christ, can lead to results greater, happier and longer lasting than a glorious campaign crowned with victories and triumphs.

I tell you, and I am right: the penitence of a conquered country, if it is continual, and if it moves from place to place like the Forty Hours,[15] will bring the conqueror to his knees in less than a year. O my God, through the divine grace, influence, power and goodness of Jesus Christ, grant me the will, the courage, the resolution I need to fast and to do what is pleasing to You.

Prophecies

"The Dominion is elected" *(in English)*.

The angel of the Lord said to me: "At four o'clock, twenty hours from now."

October 21, 1885

Captain Deane comes to give me news about the intervention

15. A Catholic devotional exercise.

of the United States. I reply: "It is a pleasure for me that you should come and tell me" *(in English)*.

Father André leaves my cell. He has his parcel under his arm. I tell him, "The greatest glory of God."

October 24, morning

"In ten days."
"Ten days from now."
"Ten days."

The Lord of Life has come to inspect His realm. His word, His blessing, His goodness are life itself. They even come to me! I fell to my knees, and the blessing of my Lord reposed upon me.

Blessing of my Lord, you descend from heaven like a fine rain which quickly soaks everything.

Blessing of my Lord, you are more beautiful to see coming from on high than the shooting stars.

Blessing of my Lord, you make me feel as good as a roaring fire does a traveller who, having stopped a little before midday, lights a campfire to warm himself and cook his dinner.

O my God! Deign to remember that the priest Frederick Eberschweiler, an ordained priest of the holy Church of Jesus Christ, blessed me together with my wife and children and Gabriel Dumont, according to the intentions of Your Providence which we love even when they surpass our understanding. Now, O my God, we need the benefit of Your paternal mercy; for my wife lies on a sickbed, and a few days ago she was in danger. And as for me — O my God, I am condemned to death!

Lord, do not let the flame of our life go out. You who have lighted it, keep it bright and shining, through Jesus Christ.

The Father of earth and heaven has inspired the following letter to the curé of St. Norbert.[16]

The enterprise which My beloved son carried out at Red River

16. Father Ritchot.

in '69 and on the Saskatchewan in '85 rests on prayer and faith.

One cannot compare the results he obtained to what he might have gotten by another course of action; for other methods are too restricted to be able to produce such great effects. They are certainly incapable of leading to results like those which the Church and men of good will now have the joy of seeing with their own eyes. Moreover, there is no point in speculating about the effects of a course of action which My beloved son had no chance to adopt.

Father Jean Tissot, Oblate of Mary Immaculate, enjoys eternal peace and happiness.

Those who were doing evil and whose influence ran like the waters of the Rio Grande are all at once dried up. With the little public influence they have left, they retrace the evil steps they have taken. Their power is shrinking to nothing. They are using their remaining power to try to repair the evil they have caused.

By contrast, the man who has prayed and who has believed marches in safety over the hills. His influence is felt, it grows, it overflows its bounds like a river whose waters rise above its banks. He is truly the one who has prayed and who has believed. His tremendous power is not stopped by the dike built to restrain it. It makes its own path amidst the good and those whom it protects. In its wake it carries the wicked hothead who, not wanting to disappear, tries to hold himself above water in the great tide of public opinion which prayer and faith have produced. But it is in vain; an irresistible force carries him away.

The Métis, with their little rifle pits hollowed out like caves in the soil of Saskatchewan, come and go without worry.

And the powerful men who wanted to devour them do not know where to turn. Where are they? I don't see any more of them. Not even a single one shows himself. Where are they?

The Spirit of God makes me see a man who invites me to the United States. Who is it who signals to me from the direction of the United States?

Saints are easy to recognize. They approach you openly.

You will not find them devious. They go straight to their target. They are prudent. They are careful. But they are neither secretive nor deceptive. They speak clearly. Wisdom is evident in their bearing. They do not talk about trivialities. They are upright. Composure is one of the distinctive traits of their character. Even their appearance causes joy. Their words, their visits leave sweet and lasting joy where they have been. Hold them in reverence.

Revelations of October 17–18, 1885

The angel of life came towards me. He said, "They went to communion today." He let me know that my dear relatives were devoting themselves whole-heartedly to performing that life-giving act. The angel carried life within himself. He was filled with it. I could see the abundance of life in him. He was calm and peaceful. Oh how beautiful are the lips of the holy angels! The lips of him who goes to communion and of her who receives the Eucharist are beautiful and stand out in the eyes of men and in the sight of heaven.

I am condemned to death, but the angel of life comes to me.

Human justice still leaves me eight days to live. But I have learned from the visit of my guardian angel that, by the grace of God, I have more time than that left on this earth! Blessed be God! Blessed be the Lord Jesus Christ!

God wants each season of the year to begin with the solemn celebration of the feasts of the four Evangelists. Saint Luke's feast should be the first day of autumn, Saint John's the first day of winter, Saint Mark's the first day of spring, Saint Matthew's the first day of summer.

"The result, not only bad but even...." That is what the Lord said to me. Men, whatever state you are in, when you have to run the risk of words or acts of pride, laziness, boastfulness, of any vice at all, of faults, of scandal, of rudeness, study the warning that the Good Lord gives you today through me, as I say, "The result, not only bad but even...."

I woke up saying the rosary. I interpreted this to mean that

I need to pray. I took my beads, and did not stop until I had recited the glorious rosary of Immaculate Mary.

Do the same, all you who have sins to atone for, graces to obtain, dangers to avoid, misfortunes to prevent.

The Spirit of God told me, "They are going to speak to you about the documents."

The Spirit of God told me, speaking of the crescent of the Turks, "They have chosen something fine."

Vision

I saw the moon in its first quarter. The weather was neither clear nor cloudy but overcast, I would say. It was not night but daytime. It was calm.

I did not see anything out of the ordinary during that phase of the moon. Nevertheless, I cannot fail to mention the joy which the first quarter of the moon brought with it. As well as I could see to predict, "it is a joy which will last about three days, I think." Blessed be God, the author of that joy. It is a joy which comes from on high, a joy which must be regarded as celestial. Its reflection will last a long time.

That joy will be celebrated for three days, but I see it increase even beyond that. At first it does not seem so splendid. But while you gaze, it increases in intensity. In a relatively short space of time it has broken all bounds and has spread far and wide.

Am I mistaken? No, this joy will take possession of all countries. It is the joy of the whole world!

The meaning of this lunar rhapsody is anything but clear. Perhaps a clue is furnished by a pun on the name of George Etienne Cartier which Riel has incorporated into the text. Instead of "Quartier de la lune" (quarter of the moon), Riel wrote "Cartier de la lune" (pronounced exactly the same). Cartier, it will be remembered, conducted the negotiations with Riel's delegation in 1870 which led to the admission of Manitoba into Confederation as a province. Riel, with his pun on Cartier's name, may wish to suggest that his own first great success, the attainment of provincial status for Manitoba, is only "the first quarter of the moon," that is, the initial phase of an even more illustrious career.

God spoke to me of the blessing given to me by my mother. Who could count all the intimate, miraculous and splendid graces which my mother's blessing brings? The blessing of the gentle heart of my mother is wonderful in all its consequences.

Above all, Saint Paul excelled in his understanding of the mentality of his own age.

He was a great genius. His devotion to Jesus Christ could not have been greater. He died for the love of the Saviour. Nevertheless, although he knew how to win the hearts of men as a missionary, he was not so pleasing to God as a minister of the liturgy. Today, we cannot imagine the prodigious ascendancy Saint Paul exercised over the faithful during his lifetime. If you want further details of the revelations given to me about the "Apostle of the Gentiles," go ask the Reverend Father J.-B. Primeau. He is the one to whom I entrusted a substantial part of my writings, in which I mention Saint Paul. When the time comes, the world will see what one must think of Saint Paul in order to please God.

The Lord wants the pagan name of the Atlantic to be discarded and replaced by that of "Saul-Paul." If nations and navigators will adopt this glorious name, the ocean will be less stormy, says the Lord. Storms will cause fewer shipwrecks. And those who cross the ocean while commending themselves to the intercession of Saint Paul will suffer less seasickness.

God wants the Pacific Ocean to bear the name of the chief of the Apostles and to be called "the Simon-Peter."

God wants the moon to bear the name of Saint Michael the Archangel and to be called "the Holy Archangel."

It is the will of God that the name of the sun be changed to a shorter, holier, more beautiful and more majestic name.

The names which the stars have today have almost all been sullied by idolatry. They are displeasing to God. And if the human race agrees to reject these profane names, to replace them with names more suitable to the harmonious relationships which ought to exist between man and his Creator, with names cloaked in the grace of redemption, fewer misfortunes will -strike the universe. Benedictions will descend on us from on high like the dew of heaven.

God wants the planet Venus to change its name and be called "Maria."

God wants the planet Mercury to be called "Anna."

God wants the planet Mars to be called "Julia."

God wants the planet Jupiter to be called "Marguerite-Marie."

God wants Neptune to be called "Catherine-Aurélie."

God wants the planet Uranus to be called "Josepha."

God wants the Big Dipper to be called the "Fabien Barnabé."

God wants the North Star to be called "Henrietta."

God wants the planet Saturn to be called "Sophia."

God wants the Morning Star to be called "Damase-Carrière."

God wants the galaxy to be called "the galaxy of the Grey Sisters." In everyday speech, when one refers to the galaxy, one should say, "the Grey Sisters."

The names in this series are all derived from the names of Riel's family, relatives, friends or benefactors.

God wants the sun to bear the name of "Jean" for the sake of the angelic forerunner,[17] of Saint John the Evangelist, of Saint John Chrysostom and of the other great saints who have borne this illustrious name. But in order to give the pronunciation of this name a greatness equal to its glory, God inspires me to put an acute accent on the letter "e" in the word "Jéan." God wants "Jéan," pronounced "Jean," to be the name of the most glorious of the stars. This name should only be given to the star of the day. Instead of saying "the sun rises," etc., one should say, "the Jéan rises," etc.

The Holy Spirit does not want the name of "Jean" to be pronounced or written with an acute accent when it is used as a baptismal name, as the name of a person or of anything other

17. John the Baptist.

than the sun. And if anyone intentionally disobeys His desire, that disobedience will be punished. You will see the punishment.

The Indians of the northern part of this continent are of Jewish origin.

The Indians of the south of this continent are Egyptians.

A ship of Egyptian merchants, with some Hebrew slaves on board, went astray around the time when the children of Jacob were wandering in the desert under the leadership of Moses.

That lost ship discovered this continent.

The Egyptian masters, less numerous than their slaves, could no longer control them; once on dry land, they had to give them their freedom. The only condition was that the masters chose to settle in the south, while they gave the Jews the opportunity to move north.

The Egyptians, with their civilization, formed empires like those of Montezuma and of Peru.

But the uneducated Hebrews, newly emerged from oppression, could only lead a very primitive and simple life.

This is what the Holy Spirit revealed to me in the month of February 1876, when I was staying with my uncle John Lee in Montreal, in St. Jean-Baptiste Village.

God wants Asia to be called "Xavieria" in honour of Saint Francis Xavier.

God wants Africa to be called "Zabulonia" in honour of Zabulon, one of the children of Jacob.

God wants Europe to let its old pagan name fall into disuse, and to be called "Napoleonia" in honour of Napoleon, because he rebuilt the altars of the "Eldest Daughter."

The term "Eldest Daughter" refers to France, which is sometimes known as the "Eldest Daughter of the Church," because the Franks were the first Germanic nation to adopt Roman Catholicism.

God does not like the present name of our continent. It is not Americo who planted the cross on the soil of the New World, but Christopher Columbus. And the divine will is that this continent be called "Beautiful Columbia" in honour of the good Christian and great man who discovered it.

God wants Oceania to be called "Provencheria" in honour of Bishop Norbert Provencher, who is a great saint in Paradise.

God revealed to me that Adam and Eve did not leave Purgatory until December 8, 1875.

On December 8, 1875, Riel experienced a mystical ecstacy while attending church in Washington, D.C. Afterwards, he always considered this experience to be the inauguration of his mission as a prophet. In saying that Adam and Eve were released from purgatory on the same day, he is stressing the world-historical importance of his mission.

God revealed to me that the great Henry IV is lost, that his soul is in the abyss for not having been sincere and because his conduct was immoral.

God revealed to me that Bolivar is in Paradise as well as Moreno.

God revealed to me that Archbishop Ignace Bourget is almost a thousand times holier than Saint Ignatius Loyola. And yet Saint Ignatius Loyola is one of the greatest saints in Paradise.

The Roman emperor Augustus is not in hell.

Louis XIV is in Paradise, but he was in Purgatory a long time. God wants him to be known as "the Great King of the Rosary."

God revealed to me that Charlemagne is one of the greatest saints in heaven.

The results of his career are incalculable. Above all due to the breadth of his views, due to the care which that great man exercised for the future, France will multiply herself by two in the New World.

Two and a half centuries from now, the New France of today will have a population of thirty-five million people. And she will be called the "House of Charlemagne."

Manitoba will become totally French-Canadian Métis. Five hundred years from now, her Métis population will number forty million souls. And in her turn she also will bear the joyous name of the "House of Charlemagne."

God wants Pope Leo XIII to adopt Montreal or Ville-Marie as his favourite city in the New World. He should try to come spend several months there. It will not make his health worse; on the contrary, the fatigue of the voyage and the crossing will have a salutary effect upon the personal well-being of the Servant of the Servants of Jesus Christ.

God wants Leo XIII to choose Ville-Marie for his second city. He should come to stay there as long as possible.

God wishes Leo XIII to come live in New France to hold in Montreal an ecumenical council of all bishops of the New World.

Today's large-scale immigration brings with it the strife of the Old World. The Church of this continent is now entering the arena in earnest. Gigantic combats are in store for her. She requires a powerful organization suited to her needs. That is why the presence of Leo XIII is such an absolute necessity in our midst. His hand must set the ranks of the episcopacy in order; his gaze must pass in review over the ecclesiastical legions; his words must inspire the great army of the Christians of this continent with the spirit of wisdom, as he cries "Well done! Well done!"

God wants Leo XIII to establish the societies of the New World on an unshakeable foundation. Let him designate sixty or seventy-two archbishops, bishops, archpriests, priests, deacons and laymen of solid and recognized piety. These men of enlightened religion, of sure and tested virtue, should have the mission of watching over the general condition of the Church; of spreading faith, hope and charity; and of defending the interests of the Holy Father, the sovereign pontiff of Rome, along with those of the Eternal City.

In this paragraph, as in several which follow, the phrase "sovereign pontiff of Rome" was written afterwards in the margin. Perhaps Riel, reading over what he had written, sensed some ambiguity in his words and wished to make his recently regained loyalty to Rome unmistakable.

But in order that this organization may have its own head in the New World, God also wants Leo XIII to delegate to one of the prelates of this continent the responsibility of being his agent to supervise the progress of religious affairs and of all matters of interest to the Church, and to report as best he can to the Holy Father, the sovereign pontiff of Rome, for the glory of God, for the salvation of souls and the welfare of society.

God wants Leo XIII to confer upon this prelate the title of "Greater Pontiff of the New World." This "Greater Pontiff" should always be loyal to the Holy Father. Let him live and die working for the Eternal City, Rome.

God revealed to me that Leo XIII cannot make a choice more pleasing to the Saviour of the world than to choose the Archbishop of St. Boniface, Monseigneur Alexandre-Antonin Taché, as Greater Pontiff of the continent.

God revealed to me that the Church of "Beautiful Columbia" will enjoy all kinds of prosperity for 2333 years, counting from December 8, 1875.

God revealed to me that after Archbishop Taché dies, the Greater Pontificate of the New World should be located at Ville-Marie in New France, and that it will remain there by the will of the Holy Father of the Eternal City, the pontiff of Rome, for 457 years, counting from December 8, 1875. The Greater Pontificate in the city of Montreal will be majestic and magnificent. It will uphold the honour of the Holy Father and of the Eternal City.

God revealed to me that at the end of these fifteen generations, the Holy Father of the Eternal City, the Pontiff of Rome, will return to confer the Greater Pontificate of the New World upon the successor of Archbishop Alexandre-Antonin Taché in Manitoba. He will reign there in the splendour and glory of Tabor for 1876 years.

These two periods of 457 and 1876 years are not arbitrarily chosen. Riel had an overall view of history which divided it into two great cycles of religious attainment. The first was the Judaeo-Christian era, extending from 457 B.C. (revival of Judaism under Ezra) to 1876 A.D. (the beginning of Riel's public mission). That period was itself divided into two sections, the time of Jewish preparation (457 B.C. to the birth of Christ), and the era of Christian fulfillment (the birth of Christ to 1876 A.D.). The second great historical period, internally sub-divided like the first, begins in 1876 A.D. with Riel's revelation and extends forward for 457 years while the papacy resides in Montreal, then another 1876 years when the papacy will be in St. Vital. This extended period represents God's promise and fulfillment to the new chosen people, the Métis, just as the first period represented God's promise and fulfillment to the first chosen people, the Jews.

God revealed to me that Leo XIII will cover himself with undying glory if he devotes himself to founding a New Italy in the North-West, on the east side of the Rocky Mountains. If Leo XIII really interests himself in the construction of a New Ireland, a New Bavaria, a New Poland in the huge Territory whose capital today is Regina; if Leo XIII agrees to support the foundation of a New Belgium on Vancouver Island as well as the French-Canadian-Métis colonization of Manitoba, God reveals to me that He will console his old age, that He will prolong his days and that He will make his reign forever remembered in both hemispheres. And the brilliance of his career will dazzle the whole Church.

God revealed to me that, in the designs of Providence, He has chosen the United States to protect New France and the North-West against the malevolent powers who would like to rule them.

God revealed to me that the United States are destined one day to inherit all the power and prosperity which Great Britain now possesses.

God revealed to me that the government of the United States is going to become extraordinarily powerful. Providence will use it to chastise the countries of Latin America, after their continual wars render them guilty of great sins. Then the armies of the United States will return victorious from the distant lands of the equator, loaded with wealth, a colossal glory marching with them, the wind of heaven hardly sufficing to deploy the majesty of their banners.

God revealed to me that the Spanish in the New World are like the French in "Napoleonia."

God revealed to me that the Spanish nations of our continent have the divine mission of lending a strong hand to the Greater Pontificate in New France and in Manitoba.

God showed me the grandeur of the empires which will arise on both sides of the equator.

God let me observe the cities, the towns, the states and the vast lands of the Spanish nations. Only the telescope used for the observation of the stars could have helped me discover the extent of their power. The undulations of the Spanish land were filled with glory as the waves of the ocean are filled with light when their whitecaps sparkle in the rays of the sun.

Today, if England adopts a policy of clemency, God will leave her power intact.

God revealed to me that He would be pleased to see the two Englands[18] enter into a legislative union to further their interests in commerce and world affairs.

God wants them to try the project of imperial union, at least for the limited time of one generation, with the initial understanding that the union may be peacefully dissolved in case the two countries should not succeed in making laws sufficiently general and sufficiently stable to establish harmony.

God revealed to me that disastrous wars were about to break out against England. If she doubles her strength by uniting with the United States, she will escape from many problems.

God revealed to me, on the other hand, that this sort of union with Great Britain would, more than anything else, help the United States to strengthen their trade in all parts of the world. God revealed to me that in thus uniting with the Great Republic, England could easily give Ireland more freedom; and in uniting with Great Britian, the United States would find themselves in a better position to contribute to the happiness of Ireland.

The diaries end here.

18. Great Britain and the United States.

Biographical Notes

ANDRÉ, ALEXIS. Superior of the Oblate missionaries in the Saskatchewan district, he strenuously opposed Riel's attempts to foment rebellion among the Métis. He served as Riel's confessor and spiritual director from mid August 1885 until the latter's execution.

ARCAND, JENEVIÈVE. A Métisse, probably resident at St. Peter's mission, Montana, when Riel was a teacher there in 1883-84.

AZUR, GABRIEL. Unidentified Métis, probably resident at St. Peter's mission.

BANDINI, JOSEPH. Jesuit missionary in Montana.

BARNABÉ, FABIEN. Pastor of the French-Canadian Catholic church in Keeseville, New York. Riel visited there often in the years 1874-78 and was once engaged to marry Father Barnabé's sister Evelina. The priest died in 1883.

BARCELO, PETER. Jesuit missionary in Montana, stationed in Helena and serving the Crow Indians. Riel wrongly wrote his name as "Barsalou."

BLAKE, EDWARD. Leader of the Liberal opposition in the House of Commons at the time of the Riel rebellion.

BOUCHER, JEAN-BAPTISTE. Member of the Exovedate.

BOURGET, IGNACE. Bishop of Montreal, 1840-76, and titular archbishop of Martianapolis, 1876-85. Riel interpreted Bourget's interest in and encouragement of him as proof of the validity of his prophetic mission. Under Riel's new religious dispensation, Bourget would have occupied the position of first pope of the New World.

BOYER, WILLIAM. A Métis who was associated with Charles Nolin in the last-minute attempt to prevent the rebellion. He was arrested by Riel, but was not sentenced to death like Nolin, whom Riel considered the true organizer of opposition to him.

BROADWATER, C.A. Proprietor of a large trading company in Montana. Riel was affiliated with Broadwater's rival, the T.C. Power Company. Also, Colonel Broadwater was a force in the

Democratic Party, whereas Riel sided with the Republicans in local politics.

BRONDEL, JOHN B. Bishop of Helena at the time Riel was in Montana. He was a member of the secular clergy, not a Jesuit.

BURSTON, MAGNUS. A Métis residing near Duck Lake. He worked at Hillyard Mitchell's store and was present when Riel's men pillaged it on March 25, 1885. On October 10-12, Burston was tried in Regina for treason-felony, but was acquitted for lack of positive evidence.

CARRIÈRE, DAMASE. Member of the Exovedate, killed at the battle of Batoche.

CATALDO, JOSEPH M. Jesuit superior-general of the Rocky Mountain missions at the time Riel was in Montana.

CATHERINE-AURÉLIE, MOTHER. Foundress of the Soeurs Adoratrices du Précieux Sang in St. Hyacinthe, Quebec. Riel regarded her very highly, crediting her with the semi-miraculous cure of one of his sisters. In 1883 he made a donation of land to the convent in return for perpetual remembrance in the prayers of the nuns.

COCHIN, LOUIS. An Oblate missionary, he was one of Riel's confessors in July and August, 1885. Along with Father Fourmond, he persuaded Riel to recant his heresies.

DAMIANI, JOSEPH. A Jesuit missionary in Montana, based at St. Peter's mission. He performed Riel's marriage in 1882.

DEANE, R. BURTON. British career officer who had joined the North West Mounted Police. As commander of the Regina detachment in 1885, he was responsible for custody of Louis Riel.

DEARBORN, THOMAS. Unidentified.

DELORME, JOSEPH. A Métis participant in the rebellion but not one of the leaders. Convicted of treason-felony, he was released on his own recognizance.

DUGAS, GEORGES. Missionary stationed at St. Boniface. He gave sympathy and advice to Riel during the insurrection of 1869-70. Later he authored several books on the history of the North-West.

DUMAS, MICHEL. One of the principal Métis in the rebellion, although not a member of the Exovedate. Together with Gabriel Dumont, he escaped to the United States after the fall of Batoche. Like Dumont, he also spent some time in Buffalo Bill's Wild West show.

DUMONT, EDOUARD. The younger brother of Gabriel Dumont.

DUMONT, GABRIEL. Military leader of the rebellion with the title of adjutant-general.

DUMONT, ISIDORE. Older brother of Gabriel Dumont killed at the battle of Duck Lake. Not to be confused with their father Isidore, who played no role in the rebellion.

EBERSCHWEILER, FREDERICK. Jesuit missionary in Montana, stationed at Fort Benton. He blessed Riel and Gabriel Dumont as they were returning to Canada in June 1885. The blessing had a powerful impact on both of them, making them think that God would support their cause. Riel usually wrote his name "Ebersville."

FORGEZ, JOHN FRANKLIN. Unidentified.

FOURMOND, JEAN-VITAL. Cure of the church of St. Laurent, across the river from Batoche. Riel was able to manipulate this sympathetic and rather naïve priest to gain support for his cause, although of course the rebellion meant an open break between them. Father Fourmond was at Regina in July and August 1885 to testify at Riel's trial. Along with Father Cochin he succeeded in obtaining Riel's abjuration.

GARIÉPY, PHILIPPE. Métis follower of Riel. Not a member of the Exovedate, but sentenced to seven years hard labour for his part in the rebellion.

GARIÉPY, PIERRE. Son-in-law of Cuthbert Grant, the famous Métis leader of an earlier era. Gariepy became a member of the Exovedate and was sentenced to three years imprisonment after the rebellion.

GARNOT, PHILIPPE. A French-Canadian resident at Batoche. Although not really sympathetic to the rebellion, he was pressed into service as secretary of the Exovedate because he could read and write. He was convicted of treason-felony and sentenced to seven years imprisonment, but was released after serving one year.

GIORDA, JOSEPH. Jesuit missionary in Montana, died August 1882. Riel wrote his name "Giudi."

GRANDIN, VITAL. Bishop of the diocese of St. Albert, which included the Batoche area, at the time of the rebellion. In September 1884 he visited Batoche, where he heard the grievances of Riel and the Métis.

IMODA, JOHN B. Jesuit missionary in Montana, stationed at the cathedral church in Helena from 1880 to 1886.

IRVINE, A.G. Commissioner of the North West Mounted Police during the rebellion. When rumours of trouble reached Regina in mid March of 1885, Irvine marched north with 100 men to reinforce the small garrison at Prince Albert. Thereafter he and his men sat in that city until the fall of Batoche, playing no military role except as a possible threat to Riel. Because of this passivity, Irvine's name came under a cloud after the rebellion, and he soon resigned his command.

JACKSON, THOMAS EASTWOOD. Older brother of W.H. Jackson. T.E. Jackson was, at the beginning, a collaborator of his brother and of Riel in drafting a petition of grievances to send to Ottawa. However, unlike his brother, he did not support the rebellion. Riel made him a prisoner at Batoche when Jackson came there to try to secure his brother's release. He gave damaging testimony against Riel at the latter's trial.

JACKSON, WILLIAM HENRY. Secretary of the Settlers' Union of Prince

Albert, Jackson played an important part in securing white support for Riel in the early, constitutional phase of the movement. He then became a religious enthusiast, joining Riel's new cult. The latter seems to have come to regard him as deranged and kept him in custody during the rebellion. Jackson was tried for treason-felony but acquitted by reason of insanity. He soon escaped from the Selkirk asylum and went to the United States, where he had a long career as a socialist organizer.

JOBIN, JOSEPH. A Métis who arrived at Batoche on May 1, 1885, with an encouraging message from the Indians and half-breeds of the Battle River area, who had risen in revolt and plundered the town of Battleford.

LAFONTAINE, CALIXTE. Métis follower of Riel, not a member of the Exovedate.

LAFRAMBOISE, AUGUSTE. A relative of Gabriel Dumont, whose mother came from the Laframboise clan.

LANGEVIN, HECTOR. Minister of Public Works in the federal cabinet at the time of the rebellion.

LARANCE, CHARLIE. Unidentified Métis.

LAROCQUE. The reference is probably to B. Larocque, an otherwise undistinguished Métis follower of Riel whose name appears once in the captured rebel papers.

LEE, JOHN. The husband of Riel's aunt Lucie (his father's sister). The Lees lived in Mile End, a suburb of Montreal. John Lee was a businessman of modest prosperity and a local alderman. In February 1876, the date referred to in the diary, Lee was virtually holding Riel under private arrest because of the latter's alleged insanity. Shortly thereafter, Lee had his nephew committed to the Longue-Pointe lunatic asylum.

LEO XIII. Pope of the Roman Catholic Church at the time of the rebellion.

LÉPINE, MAXIME. Brother of Ambroise-D. Lépine, who was Riel's military commander in 1869-70 and who was subsequently tried for the murder of Thomas Scott. Maxime Lépine and Charles Nolin initially were Riel's closest confidants after his arrival at Batoche in July 1884. Maxime became a member of the Exovedate and was convicted of treason-felony after the rebellion.

LESTANC, J.-J.-M. Catholic missionary priest in the North-West. He was administrator of the Diocese of St. Boniface during 1869-70 while Bishop Taché was attending the Ecumenical Council at Rome.

MACKAY, TOM. Scottish half-breed resident in Prince Albert. Having been an eyewitness to the outbreak of the rebellion, Mackay gave important testimony against Riel at the trial. I have been unable to find any other information about Mackay's visit to Batoche as mentioned in Riel's diary on April 30, 1885.

MACKENZIE, ALEXANDER. Liberal prime minister of Canada, 1874-78. Mackenzie's government granted Riel's amnesty in 1875 on condition of five years' banishment from Canada. Riel always wrote his name as "McKenzie."

MARGUERITE-MARIE, BLESSED. Marguerite-Marie Alocoque, a French nun of the seventeenth century who was beatified in 1864. When Riel's sister Sara was critically ill in 1872, she recovered after praying to Marguerite-Marie, whereupon she adopted the name of her heavenly patron and became Sister Marguerite-Marie. Because of this cure, which was considered a miracle by those who witnessed it, Riel had a special devotion to the Blessed Marguerite-Marie and to the cult of the Sacred Heart of Jesus of which she was the greatest proponent.

MARGUERITE-MARIE, SISTER. Louis Riel's sister Sara, who became a Grey nun in 1868. She went as a missionary sister to Ile-a-la-crosse, where she died in 1883. Although Louis and Sara were separated physically for most of their lives, they were unusually close in spirit.

MARIE-ANNE. As Riel had no sister of this name, the reference must be to an otherwise unknown sister of Riel's wife, Marguerite née Monette.

MIDDLETON, FREDERICK D. British career officer who in 1884 became commander of the Canadian militia, with the rank of major-general. He commanded all military operations in 1885, and personally led the force that took Batoche.

MONETTE, MARGUERITE. Maiden name of Louis Riel's wife.

MORENO, GABRIEL GARCIA. Dictator of Ecuador, 1861-75. His regime was semi-theocratic. He officially dedicated Ecuador to the protection of the Sacred Heart of Jesus.

MORTON, OLIVER PERRY. Republican senator from Indiana. In 1875 Riel sought his backing for a military venture in the Canadian North-West, but Morton refused. Riel then offered to pray God to heal the legs of Senator Morton, who was a paraplegic, confined to a wheelchair. Morton, an atheist, was not impressed by this offer. When Riel learned of Morton's death (November 1, 1877), he began to pray that God would resurrect the senator from the grave to aid him in the North-West.

MOULIN, JULIEN. Oblate missionary, pastor of St. Antoine-de-Padua Church near Batoche.

NEAULT, ANDRÉ (or Nault). A cousin of Louis Riel, French-Canadian by blood but a Métis for all practical purposes. He was an important figure in the events of 1869-70. It was on his farm in October 1869 that the first act of resistance occurred, when a band of Métis, led by Riel, prevented the Canadian surveyors from carrying out their work. Nault was a member of the court martial that sentenced Thomas Scott to death. He was later tried for murder but acquitted by a hung jury. Nault, unlike many Métis, did not move away from the Red River area and was not involved in the 1885 rebellion.

NEAULT, NAPOLEON (or Nault). Son of André Nault, he moved from Red River to the Batoche area. When Riel returned to Winnipeg for a visit in June 1883 he met Napoléon, who told him of the grievances of the Métis settlers on the Saskatchewan. Nault participated in the rebellion and escaped to the United States afterward.

NOLIN, CHARLES. A cousin of Riel's and one of the more prosperous of the Métis of the Batoche area. Before moving west, he had been a cabinet minister in Manitoba. He had been one of the most active in pressing for the invitation to Riel to return to Canada, and he collaborated closely with the latter for several months in the agitation. But he was frightened by Riel's adoption of a violent strategy and attempted to prevent the rebellion at the last minute. When the Provisional Government was declared, Nolin was arrested and sentenced to death, whereupon he swore his allegiance to Riel and was pardoned. As soon as he had a chance, Nolin escaped from Batoche and found refuge in Prince Albert. After the rebellion, he gave damning evidence at Riel's trial.

OUELLETTE, JOSEPH. One of the more militant Métis, he was the father of Moïse Ouellette.

OUELLETTE, MOÏSE. Brother-in-law of Gabriel Dumont and member of the Exovedate. He voted against the resolutions of the Exovedate which officially declared Riel a prophet and which set up Saturday as the Sabbath. Hence Riel's plea in the diary that God enlighten Ouellette and change his thinking.

OUIMET, J.-ALDÉRIC. Colonel Ouimet was commander of the 65th Carabiniers Mont-Royal, who served in the North-West Rebellion campaign. Actually the 65th did not march with Middleton but were sent to Alberta under General Thomas B. Strange. Ouimet, a Conservative M.P., had been a friend and supporter of Riel in the 1870s.

PALLADINO, LAWRENCE. Jesuit missionary in Montana, secretary to Bishop Brondel. Author of *Indian and White in the Northwest* (1894).

PEPIN, SIMON. A Métis Agent of the C.A. Broadwater Company in Montana. In 1882-83 Riel attempted to prosecute Pepin for selling liquor to the Métis; but the case was dismissed because there was no legal bar to the possession of alcohol by half-breeds. Riel lost all his money in the case.

PRANDO, PETER PAUL. Jesuit missionary in Montana, known as the "Apostle of the Crows."

PRIMEAU, JEAN-BAPTISTE. Pastor of Notre-Dame-des-Canadiens in Worcester, Massachusetts, during the 1870s. Riel visited Father Primeau several times in 1874-75. Toward the end of the latter year, Primeau played a key role in putting Riel under virtual private arrest and sending him to Canada, where he was eventually put into an insane asylum.

PROVENCHER, NORBERT. The first bishop of St. Boniface, he baptized Louis Riel.

RIEL, CHARLES. Louis Riel's younger brother, nicknamed "Meunier." He died of an infection in November 1875, shortly before his twenty-first birthday.

RIEL, JEAN. Louis Riel's son, born May 9, 1882, in Montana. He died in an auto accident in 1908 without leaving any descendants.

RIEL, MARGUERITE. Louis Riel's wife, nee Marguerite Monette. She was the illiterate daughter of a Métis hunter living in Montana. Married at twenty-one, she died of consumption at the age of twenty-five, six months after her husband's execution.

RITCHOT, JOSEPH-NOËL. Cure of the parish of St. Norbert in the Red River colony at the time of the first rebellion. Ritchot helped Riel with sympathy and advice, then went to Ottawa as part of the delegation that negotiated the entry of Manitoba into Confederation. For years afterward, he remained a close friend and correspondent of Riel. (Curiously, Riel wrote his name as Joseph-Norbert, perhaps unconsciously conflating it with the name of Ritchot's parish.)

ROSS, JOHN. Métis follower of Riel, not a member of the Exovedate.

SAINTE-THERÈSE, SISTER. A Grey sister, living in their convent at St. Norbert. She was present at the death of Louis Riel's father, who gave her a special blessing for his son. She passed this on to him on May 3, 1873. Riel considered this posthumous paternal benediction to be an important proof of the validity of his divine mission.

SAUSEL, FREDERICK. Unidentified.

TACHÉ, ALEXANDRE-ANTONIN. Oblate missionary, bishop (1853-71) and archbishop (1871-94) of St. Boniface. Taché was Louis Riel's first and most important patron. He arranged for Riel to study at the Collège de Montréal; later he tried to mediate between Riel and the federal government and to secure him an amnesty for the Scott affair. In his new religion, Riel wished to put Taché in the role of "greater pontiff of the New World," replacing Mgr. Ignace Bourget, who died June 8, 1885. The writings of the last few months of Riel's life, after he abjured his heresies, are characterized by an exaggerated deference to Taché.

TAILLEFER, JOSEPH. Native of Quebec who, after having been a Papal Zouave, came to Manitoba in 1870 as a captain in Wolseley's expeditionary force. Settling in the west, he was elected member of the provincial legislature for Ste. Agathe in 1878.

TAYLOR, JAMES W. American consul in Winnipeg. He collaborated with Riel in the events of 1869-70. Riel wrote to Taylor shortly after arriving in Saskatchewan in 1884 in an indirect bid for American sympathy and support in the agitation. During and after his trial, Riel tried through Taylor to get the United States government to intervene on his behalf, but without success.

TCHEKIKAM. Probably the Cree Indian, identified at Riel's trail as "Chic-i-cum," who brought Poundmaker a letter from Riel, written after the battle of Duck Lake, requesting help in the rebellion.

TISSOT, JEAN. Oblate priest stationed at St. Boniface.

TOUROND. The name of a numerous Métis family which lived south of Batoche. Fish Creek was also known locally as "Tourond's Coulée.

TRUDEL, FRANCOIS-XAVIER. A Conservative senator of ultramontane sympathies. He was a strong supporter of the movement to obtain an amnesty for Riel in the 1870s. After the rebellion of 1885, he became a member of the Riel Defence Committee.

TURCOTTE, NORBERT. Métis follower of Riel, not a member of the Exovedate.

VANDALE, BAPTISTE. Métis follower of Riel in the rebellion. Although not a member of the Exovedate, he was convicted of treason-felony and sentenced to seven years' imprisonment, of which he served a year before being paroled.

Appendix:
Description of the Manuscripts

The material which I have arranged into seven chapters according to chronology is contained in four separate notebooks and one loose sheet of paper. These documents are described below.

A. One paperbound, pocket-sized note pad about three-quarters of an inch thick, now the property of the Public Archives of Canada, in the collection entitled Ministry of Justice, Documents Relating to Louis Riel and the North-West Rebellion, 1873-1886. RG 13 B2, Vol. 11, pages 1839-2104.

This notebook presents certain difficulties because Riel apparently used it at widely separated times and did not make all entries in chronological order. From considerations of internal evidence and from examination of the colours of ink and pencil used in the book, I have arrived at certain conclusions which appear defensible but are not demonstrable beyond all doubt. These conclusions are the basis of my arrangement of the material into chapters.

Chapter 1 consists of pages 2070-2096. These pages are clearly dated June 1884, and all are written in the same shade of blue ink.

Chapter 2 (except for the first paragraph) consists of pages 1839-1900, written in pencil, plus pages 1901-2057, written in brown ink. The latter contain mention of only one date: February 13, 1885. Probably the pages were all composed during the winter of 1884-85, but there is no way to be more specific about the date. I have also assumed that the pencilled pages stem from this same period, since they deal with similar themes and are, to a considerable extent, rough drafts of the material found in the brown ink pages.

Chapter 3 consists of pages 2097-2103, also written in brown ink. This section is set off from all other entries in the notebook by a number of blank pages before and after. Assessment of the contents permits positive dating to March 1885.

Chapter 5 is composed of pages 2058-2069, written in a blue-black ink which is very little, if at all, different from the ink found on the pages immediately following (that is, pages 2070-2096, which I have called Chapter 1). The dating of pages 2058-2069 must be considered uncertain. They clearly bear consecutive dates from May 16 through May 24, but nowhere is there mention of a year. Do they belong to 1884 or 1885? In favour of the former year, one must admit that they are immediately followed by pages 2070-2096, written in similar ink, which unquestionably come from June 1884. In support of 1885, one can argue that the dates May 16-24 correspond perfectly to Riel's trip from Batoche to Regina. Furthermore, the mood of extreme depression and resignation is understandable in view of the crushing defeat of Batoche, although it is curious that the pages contain no direct reference to these events. Another point is the reference to Manitoba and Winnipeg, which accords with the government's original intention to send Riel there for detention and trial. In May of 1884, he made no trip to Manitoba. Finally, on a torn page at the very front of the book, far from these pages, there is the date May 24, 1884, written in English. This suggests that if Riel did make entries during May 1884, they were in English and in a different location in the diary from the material under consideration. All these considerations have led me to prefer the year 1885, without, however, being entirely certain.

If this argument is correct, Riel had the notebook in his possession until his internment in the NWMP gaol at Regina. It was then taken from him to be added to the other rebel papers which the Crown attorneys were to use in preparing their case against him. As it turned out, this diary played no role in the trial, but it remained with the other papers among the records of the Ministry of Justice until passing into the keeping of the Public Archives of Canada. Except for the declaration of March 5, 1885, which I have called a "revolutionary oath," the contents of this diary have not been mentioned or cited in the publications of scholars other than myself.

B. An account ledger used as a diary by Riel during the North-West Rebellion. The first fifty-seven pages are filled with consecutive entries; in addition there are two torn pages at the very end of the volume. The contents of the diary make up chapter 4 of this volume, with one exception: I have assigned the first paragraph of the diary, which begins "I have seen Bishop Grandin...," to chapter 2, because that entry must have been made around the beginning of September 1884, when Grandin visited the area. In the manuscript, this entry is set off by several drawn lines from the following material, perhaps suggesting a substantial lapse of time. This hypothesis might have received further support had I been able to examine the ink(s) on the original page; but unfortunately, I was not able to obtain access to the manuscript while preparing this book. I was compelled to work from a photocopy of the diary held in the Provincial Archives of Manitoba. The reasons for this regrettable state of affairs are of considerable interest and call for a discussion of the history of the manuscript.

When Batoche fell on May 12, the first officer to enter the council chamber of the rebels was Major George Holmes Young of the Winnipeg Field Battery. He found there a large quantity of books and papers which he tied together and sent for safe-keeping to his immediate commander, Major Edward Jarvis. As other papers turned up, Major Young took possession of them also and passed them on to Jarvis. The whole collection was then taken to Prince Albert, packed in a stout box, and sent to Ottawa on May 28 or 29. These documents became an important basis of the prosecution's case against Riel. After the trial they were preserved by the Ministry of Justice and are now housed in the Public Archives of Canada.

It is not known exactly when or where Riel's diary was discovered, but it too went to Prince Albert. However, it did not travel onward to Ottawa. For reasons unknown, it remained in Prince Albert in the joint possession of Joseph Dudley Hanafin, an ex-mounted policeman turned real estate agent, and Alexander Stewart, a local merchant whose Winnipeg relatives had once known Riel. Stewart, who knew French, set about making a partial translation into English. This task must have been completed during June, for in July the translation, as well as the original French text, began to appear in the eastern newspapers. In the meantime, Major Jarvis took the original diary with him when he returned home to Winnipeg.

All of this was highly irregular, to say the least. The diary was the personal property of Riel, and no private individual had a right to it. Jarvis should have handed it over to the Ministry of Justice to join the other papers collected at Batoche; but he must have wanted a souvenir, or perhaps he thought the journal would become valuable some day.

Another mysterious aspect of the affair is that neither the prosecution nor the defence in Riel's trial tried to subpoena the document (although Riel referred to it in his speech to the jury). Since the chief issue at the trial was whether or not the defendant was sane at the time of the rebellion, one would think his private diary, kept in those very days, would have constituted highly relevant evidence. The trial did not begin until July 24, by which time the diary had appeared almost in full in the Toronto *Globe*, together with the information that the original was in the possession of Major Jarvis; but attorneys from neither side made any effort to obtain the document.

After the rebellion, Jarvis went on to join the NWMP. He died in 1894, leaving the Winnipeg bank of Alloway and Champion as executors of his estate. The bank retained possession of a number of

Jarvis's own diaries, but it is not known for sure whether the Riel volume was still among them. Shortly after World War One, the Jarvis diaries, which were about to be thrown out, were saved from destruction by a local history buff, who donated them to the Provincial Archives of Manitoba more than three decades later. In the meantime, Riel's diary, if it ever had been with the Jarvis papers, disappeared.

It did not surface until April 6, 1970, when Eric Wells, former editor of the Winnipeg *Tribune* and history enthusiast, brought it to the Provincial Archives of Manitoba for examination. When its validity was established beyond reasonable doubt, Mr. Wells offered to sell it to the Archives on behalf of the owner, whose agent he claimed to be; but he would not reveal the identity of the owner, nor divulge any information about where the manuscript had been all these years. Under the circumstances, the Archives did not feel able to conclude the purchase, fearing that their title might not be legally secure. Mr. Wells was compelled to look elsewhere for a buyer, resulting in the much-touted auction of April 22, 1971.

The diary now reposes in a bank vault in Edmonton where it lies as security on the loan which the owners took out to purchase it and which they are still paying off. Although the diary itself is not accessible to researchers, its contents are available in the form of a bilingual text prepared under the supervision of Mr. Wells and published in 1970 as part of the Manitoba Centennial celebrations. My translation has been prepared from that text as corrected through word-by-word comparison against a photocopy of the manuscript. This process of correction was necessary because the 1970 text, prepared as it was in great haste, contains a number of errors in both the French and English versions.

C. Two diaries now the property of the Provincial Archives of Manitoba, Louis Riel Collection, Nos. 525 and 526. The latter, which stems from August 1885, makes up chapter 6 of this volume; the former, from October 1885, constitutes chapter 7.

The August diary is a ruled notebook, approximately 8″ x 6½″. It is completely written from cover to cover, though many pages have been torn out. After the preface, which takes up a page in itself, all pages have been consecutively numbered in Riel's hand from 1 to 148. The appearance of the ink, plus the fact that there are no disruptions in the numbering due to missing pages, suggest that the enumeration was done after completion of the diary, perhaps at the time the preface was added. Quite probably, Riel intended the diary to be published in some form. This impression is strengthened by seeing the very careful and thorough way in which Riel erased or blotted out certain words, sentences and paragraphs.

The October diary is a clothbound account ledger of approximately the same physical dimensions as the August diary. It also is written on every page, including the front and back covers. However, the pages are not numbered, and the manuscript does not give the same impression of meticulous care as the August *carnet*. Obviously, entries have not been made in strict chronological order.

The history of these two diaries is of some interest. Riel wrote extensively in prison and hoped that this material might be published. Before his death, he signed a will in which he named Father Alexis André, his confessor, as literary executor with rights of publication. Immediately after the execution, Father André succeeded in getting all, or almost all, of Riel's papers, thus keeping them away from Dr. Augustus Jukes, Riel's physician in Regina, who wished to submit the dead man's writings to psychiatric investigation. But Father André wanted no further controversy. Instead of making Riel's papers available to the public, he took them to the office of the Archdiocese of St. Boniface, where Archbishop Taché kept them in private custody.

In 1932, heirs of the Riel family petitioned to have these papers returned. A few documents were retained by the Archdiocese, but most were returned, although the chancellor prudently arranged for typed copies to be made before release. Some of the released documents have now disappeared, but fortunately the two diaries were acquired by the Provincial Archives of Manitoba.

This is the first occasion on which these diaries have appeared in English except in brief citations in historical works. Substantial French excerpts were published by Rossell Vien in "Louis Riel: Journal de Prison," *Ecrits du Canada Francais, XIII* (Montréal, 1962), pages 329-353.

D. One sheet of paper, written on two sides, in the Archives of the College de Montreal. I have put this page, dated October 2, 1885, at the beginning of Chapter 7, which contains the October diary from the Provincial Archives of Manitoba. This seemed particularly appropriate since the first date in that latter volume is October 3. It may even be that the single sheet now at the College was torn from the October diary; but I cannot decide that without an examination of the original manuscript page, which I have not had a chance to carry out. The translation presented here was prepared from a photocopy sent to me by the Collège.

This text has not been published before in either French or English, nor has it been mentioned in any historical work on Riel.

185

Suggestions for Further Reading

A good short treatment of the life of Riel is Hartwell Bowsfield, *Louis Riel: The Rebel and the Hero* (Toronto, 1971). Although it is now outdated and wrong in many details, Joseph Kinsey Howard's pioneering book *Strange Empire* (Toronto, 1952; republished, 1974) is still the most interesting and exciting work on Riel. The standard scholarly works remain George Stanley's two books *Louis Riel* (Toronto, 1963) and *The Birth of Western Canada* (Toronto, 1936; republished, 1961).

Desmond Morton has published a lively account of the military aspects of the rebellion, *The Last War Drum* (Toronto, 1972). The same author has also edited the transcript of Riel's trial, *The Queen v Louis Riel* (Toronto, 1974).

Those interested in Riel should not overlook George Woodcock's excellent biography of *Gabriel Dumont* (Edmonton, 1974).

Finally, on the subject of Riel's religious beliefs, I have published articles in *Journal of Canadian Studies,* Vol. 9 (August, 1974) and *Alberta History,* Vol. 23 (Winter, 1975); and an edition of Riel's writings on religion entitled *Prophetic Writings of Louis Riel* (Ottawa, National Museum of Man, 1976). These will ultimately lead to a biography stressing the religious theme.